The Take-Charge Guide to Type I Diabetes

American Diabetes Association

Publisher
Susan H. Lau

Managing Editor
Christine B. Welch

Editorial Director
Peter Banks

Associate Editor
Sherrye Landrum

Copyright © 1994 by American Diabetes Association. All rights reserved

Printed in the United States of America

American Diabetes Association
1660 Duke Street
Alexandria, Virginia 22314

Library of Congress Cataloging-in-Publication Data

The Take-charge guide to type I Diabetes
American Diabetes Association
p. cm.
Includes index.

1. Diabetes—Popular works. I. American Diabetes Association.
RC660.4.T35 1994
616.4'62–dc20 94-17538

ISBN 0-945448-35-X (pbk.)

Table of Contents

Acknowledgments

The mission of the American Diabetes Association is to prevent and cure diabetes and to improve the lives of all people affected by diabetes.

More than half of all Americans with insulin-dependent (type I) diabetes are adults 20 years old or older. Although the peak time for developing type I diabetes is in early adolescence, many people get it as adults. Regardless of how long you've had type I diabetes, as an adult, you no longer depend on someone else's decisions to determine how you will behave. For better or worse, you make your own decisions. This means that responsibility for day-to-day diabetes care is yours. We hope this book provides the information you seek about your diabetes care choices to help you make decisions that best fit your life.

Many people were asked to write about adult life with type I diabetes. They were American Diabetes Association staff members Christine B. Welch, Sherrye Landrum (who also provided page design and desktop services), and Heather Heiman, and consultants Sharon Block, Leslie Y. Dawson, Shauna S. Roberts, and Cheryl C. Ulmer. Other Association staff contributed to this book: Peter Banks; Richard Kahn, PhD; Phyllis Barrier, MS, RD, CDE; and Ted Udelson gave reviews and comments, and Carol Segree coordinated design and printing.

We are especially indebted for the reviews done by members of the Association's Professional Section. We thank Kelly Acton, MD; Sharon Buckley, RN, CDE; and Ruth Norton RN, CDE, for reviewing the book's outline. We thank David Bell, MD; David Kelley, MD; Ruth Norton, RN, CDE; Mary Beth Tierney, MD, RD; and Robin Ann Williams, MA, RD, CDE, for reviewing the book itself.

Cover design is by Wickham & Associates, Inc. Cover photo © Uniphoto.

Introduction

Diabetes Is a Take-Charge Disease

I t probably happened quickly. One day, your life was different. On that day, you learned you had insulin-dependent (type I) diabetes, the disease that doesn't go away. It was yours for life.

You may be recently diagnosed with type I diabetes, or it may be old hat to you. In either case, your concern is the same: a high quality of life. Good blood glucose control can contribute a great deal to your quality of life. Your doctor can prescribe insulin for you, your dietitian can advise you on healthy food choices, your diabetes educator can help you choose which times are best for shots and exercise, but how you use this information to control your blood glucose is up to you. Most health professionals would admit that a well-informed patient is much better at knowing what controls his or her blood glucose levels than they are. With a disease like diabetes, the person who has it is in charge from day to day.

Good diabetes control is helped along by information and putting it to use. If you read *Diabetes Forecast*, the member's magazine of the American Diabetes Association, or other diabetes-care magazines each month, you're ahead of the game in getting information. In fact, you may have more new information about diabetes treatment than a lot of family doctors. You may even find yourself teaching your health-care professionals a thing or two.

Too many people rely on doctors, parents, friends, counselors, coaches, and dietitians to tell them what to do. You don't have to. *The Take-Charge Guide to Type I Diabetes* gives you information to help you make positive, health-affirming choices about diabetes care. This book was designed to help you

✦ Put a positive spin on your diabetes care. Diabetes puts limits on your life, but not as much as you might think. Sure, you'll want to think more about what you eat, but your diet and exercise plan is really the same one that anyone who wants to be healthy and fit follows.

✦ Find answers to everyday questions. It helps to know the medical reasons that make some choices healthier for you than others. Use this information as you decide how much insulin to use before dinner, when to have a social drink, and which cold medicine to buy.

✦ Practice making healthy choices. This gives you the best chance of success at avoiding the long-term complications of diabetes. You can't completely control diabetes. That would mean curing it. What you can do, most of the time, is control how you handle your diabetes. And how you care for yourself. Making healthy choices is difficult for anyone.

Take charge of your type I diabetes in small steps. Perhaps you can start by learning more about how insulin works. Then maybe you'll want to work toward getting more flexible about when you eat and work out. What diabetes-care goals do you have in mind? How do they fit in with the goals you've set for other parts of your life? By taking charge of your diabetes, you help make diabetes just one aspect of a full, interesting life. Isn't that worth it?

One

Biology of Type I Diabetes

When you were first told you have insulin-dependent (type I) diabetes, you and your family probably had many questions about the disease. Why does my doctor think I have diabetes? Can the doctor be sure? What causes diabetes? Will I always have diabetes? Is there any chance of curing my diabetes? Will my brothers and sisters or my children get diabetes?

Not all of these questions have answers. But you can get some answers by understanding a little about the biology of type I diabetes—how the immune system works to protect the body, what goes wrong in the body with diabetes, and how doctors measure these changes.

What Is Type I Diabetes?

Diabetes is a group of diseases in which there is too much glucose (a kind of sugar) in the blood. In India, 3,000 years ago, doctors already knew there were at least two types of diabetes. Today, many types of diabetes are known. The two most common forms of the disease are insulin-dependent (type I) and non-insulin-dependent (type II) diabetes. Type I diabetes affects less than 10% of all people with diabetes.

The symptoms of type I diabetes are well defined.

Symptoms can include being very thirsty, needing to urinate frequently, losing weight even though you are hungrier than usual and eating more, feeling unusually tired, and having blurred vision. These symptoms may develop very quickly.

The early teen years are the most common time for type I diabetes to start. Thus, if you were a teenager when your symptoms first appeared, your doctor probably suspected type I diabetes right away and checked a sample of your blood to see if it had too much glucose. However, if you were a young child or an adult, your doctor may have only tested you for type I diabetes after ruling out other conditions more common in people your age. Or, if you were a tiny child, the disease may have developed so fast that you may have fallen into a coma before anyone noticed your other symptoms.

Diagnosing Diabetes

Blood tests for glucose levels are the only sure way to diagnose diabetes. Blood tests are used to diagnose both type I and type II diabetes. They are also used to diagnose gestational diabetes in pregnant women with no previous diabetes.

The simplest kind of test is called a *random plasma glucose test*. In this test, the doctor takes a sample of blood and measures glucose without asking you to fast. If you have symptoms of diabetes and the test reveals a glucose level of 200 mg/dl or more, diabetes is diagnosed.

Another test is the *fasting plasma glucose test*. In this test, one sample of your blood is drawn and tested for glucose after you have fasted for at least 6 hours. Levels less than 115 mg/dl are normal. Diabetes is diagnosed when glucose levels greater than 140 mg/dl occur in two fasting plasma glucose tests.

Sometimes, an *oral glucose tolerance test* is performed to diagnose diabetes. For this test, you must fast for at least 10 hours, usually overnight. First, your fasting blood glucose is measured. Then you drink a solution of glucose. Blood samples are taken at intervals of 30 minutes or 1 hour. The five blood samples of a person without diabetes show a low glucose level that rises after the glucose drink but then falls quickly. However, the glucose level of a person with diabetes rises to high levels and stays up for a long time. High levels in the oral glucose tolerance test are defined as 200 mg/dl or higher 2 hours after the glucose drink and in at least one other of the four blood samples after the glucose drink.

These tests may sound complex, but with them diabetes can be diagnosed precisely. If your results are too high, you have diabetes. However, your doctor must then decide whether you have type I or type II diabetes. People with type I diabetes are likely to be thin, whereas people with type II diabetes are likely to be overweight. Also, half or more of people with type I diabetes are less than 30 years old at diagnosis, whereas almost everyone with type II diabetes is older than 30 at diagnosis. Most important, people with type II diabetes have a good chance of controlling their excess glucose levels by changing their diet, exercising, and taking oral diabetes medicine. This is because they seem to have enough insulin, it just doesn't work the way it should. By contrast, people with type I diabetes don't have the insulin they need and must have injections to control their glucose level for the rest of their lives. This important distinction leads to the other common name for type I diabetes, insulin-*dependent* diabetes.

What does insulin have to do with glucose? Glucose provides energy to the body's cells. Insulin not only allows the glucose to enter the cells, but it also helps the body put glucose, protein, and fat to work. Glucose can only do its job properly if there's enough insulin in the body with it.

In people with type I diabetes, insulin-producing cells in the pancreas are damaged and stop making insulin. These cells are called *beta cells*. They are found, along with other types of cells, in a group called *islets*. Without insulin, glucose can't get into the cells, and can't be stored for future energy needs. Instead, it builds up in the blood to high levels. Some of the extra glucose coats muscle proteins and other body parts like the eye lens and joints. Some of the extra glucose may also be lost in urine, causing high glucose levels in a urine test.

Honeymoon Phase

People with type I diabetes must take insulin injections to make up for what their body no longer makes. However, some people enjoy a brief vacation, called a honeymoon phase, from needing as much or any insulin injections. The honeymoon can last for several months after diagnosis and the start of treatment. After being on insulin for a month or so, many newly diagnosed people require a lower insulin dose than they did at first. Some can even get by for a time without any insulin injections at all. However, these changes do not mean that the person is cured or was misdiagnosed. This is because your pancreas may still be able to secrete *some* insulin, but only for awhile.

Unfortunately, the loss of the insulin-producing cells continues during the honeymoon phase. After some time, perhaps up to a year, the beta cells are unable to make insulin. Gradually, after the initial decrease in their insulin dose, people with type I diabetes need to increase their insulin dose. The honeymoon phase usually lasts only a few months to a year.

How Diabetes Develops
....

Through research, we are learning about what happens in type I diabetes. We know that it is an autoimmune disease, as are many other diseases, including multiple sclerosis, rheumatoid arthritis, and lupus. In autoimmune diseases, the immune system begins attacking the body's own cells and tissues as intruders or bacteria. Which cells are damaged varies by disease.

The focus of the attack in type I diabetes is the beta cells, which produce insulin. Beta cells—and their ability to produce insulin—are eventually destroyed by the autoimmune system. The big question is, why? Scientists have already found many factors linked to diabetes: genetics, autoantibodies, viruses, cold temperatures, cows' milk, oxygen free radicals, chemicals and drugs, and young age.

✦**Genetics.** Genes, the basic units of heredity, clearly play a role in making some people more likely to get diabetes. This role can be seen because diabetes is more common among people of some races than others. For example, white people are more likely than members of other races to develop type I diabetes. The connection also shows up within families-- relatives of someone with type I diabetes have a higher risk for developing diabetes than nonrelatives.

Scientists have studied identical twins to find out how big a role genetics plays in diabetes. The genes of identical twins are the same. If one twin gets diabetes and the other doesn't, clearly something other than genes must be at work. Scientists found that in sets of twins in which one person has type I diabetes, the other twin also gets the disease at most only 25–50% of the time. This 1-in-3 risk of diabetes is 100 times the risk of the average American developing diabetes, so genes do increase a person's risk for diabetes. Yet, even when they have genes putting them at risk, half or more of the co-twins never get type I diabetes. This shows that environment also plays a big role. That at least 85% of people who develop type I diabetes have no known family history of type I diabetes backs up the role of environment.

Risks for other relatives of someone with type I diabetes are much lower. Parents of people with type I diabetes have a 5% risk of getting the disease. Siblings who aren't identical twins have a 7 to 10% risk, and their children have between a 1 and 6% risk. However, a child's risk is influenced by which parent has type I diabetes. Children are three times as likely to develop type I diabetes when their father has diabetes than when their mother does. (For more on the risks to children when a parent has diabetes, see Chapter 10.)

Researchers have found some of the genes that make a person more likely to get type I diabetes. The culprits are certain members of a set of genes called human leukocyte antigens, or HLA. HLA genes determine which molecules (antigens) sit on the surfaces of cells. It's these molecules that the immune system checks to discover which cells are foreign cells. To make things complex, people don't all have the same version of the HLA genes. In fact, there are many kinds of each. Each person inherits one kind from each parent for all HLA genes.

Of the HLA genes, the one most linked to type I diabetes is called HLA-DR. Even though there are many variants of HLA-DR, 95% of white people with type I diabetes have the DR3 form, the DR4 form, or both. This strong link suggests that DR3 and DR4 may make people more likely to get type I diabetes. Similarly, the variants of another HLA gene, HLA-DQ, variants DQw2, DQw8, or both occur in most people with type I diabetes. Thus, HLA-DQ variants may also increase the risk of diabetes.

These genes cannot be used for predicting who in the general population will get diabetes, because most people with DR3 or DR4 remain healthy. However, screening can be valuable for relatives of people with type I diabetes. A research hospital can use HLA tests to tell the odds of your relatives also getting the disease. Brothers and sisters who have the same two HLA-DR variants as you do have a 15% chance of getting type I diabetes. The risk drops to 5% for those who share just one variant with you and to less than 1% if both their HLA-DR variants are different from yours.

In the future, HLA antigens may help doctors prevent diabetes. By changing the role played by a person's HLA genes, doctors might be able to eliminate a person's tendancy to get type I diabetes.

✦**Autoantibodies**. The immune system uses both white blood cells (called *T cells*) and antibodies to kill invaders. Antibodies are made by another group of cells called *B cells*. Like the T cells, each antibody attacks only one specific invader, recognized by the shape of a molecule sitting on its surface.

Sometimes B cells produce antibodies to the body's own cells, called autoantibodies. Many are found in people with type I diabetes, but three are especially common. These are antibodies to

✦islet cells (beta cells are just one type of islet cell in the pancreas),

✦to insulin, and

✦to glutamic acid decarboxylase (also called GAD or the 64K protein). GAD is a protein produced in the beta cells.

Thus, these three autoantibodies all attack the lead characters in the drama of insulin production.

Although T cells, not autoantibodies, are the culprits in the final beta cell destruction of type I diabetes, scientists suspect that these three autoantibodies act as accessories, particularly because they are so often found loitering around the scene of the crime. Of people newly diagnosed with type I diabetes, 70 to 80% have antibodies to islet cells, 30 to 50% have antibodies to insulin, and 80 to 95% have antibodies to GAD. These antibodies may be present for years before type I diabetes develops, but often disappear afterward.

Some researchers claim that the body's immune response to it's own GAD is a primary cause of type I diabetes. It turns out that a small region of the GAD protein is almost identical to a small region of a protein on a virus named Coxsackie B4. (This virus and its sister Coxsackie viruses are cousins of the virus that causes polio.) Because these two regions probably have similar shapes, the GAD protein, which is part of the body, and the Coxsackie B4 virus, which is foreign to the body, might look alike to a T cell or antibody. According to this theory, after a Coxsackie B4 virus infection is over, the T cells produced to fight it might switch their attentions to GAD in beta cells in some people, destroying these cells and causing type I diabetes.

Because autoantibodies to islet cells, insulin, and GAD are so common in people with type I diabetes and can often be detected years before the disease actually develops, scientists are testing their use as a screening test for type I diabetes in people at high risk. For example, the risk of getting type I diabetes is much higher in relatives with high levels of antibodies to islet cells; 70% develop diabetes within 5 years. And some combinations of autoantibodies and HLA genes lead to even higher risks. Thus, research hospitals that test for autoantibodies in relatives of people with type I diabetes can often tell whose risk of the disease is low and whose is high.

These antibodies may play a role in future therapies as well. Researchers have several ideas for ways to prevent type I diabetes. Such therapies will depend on finding people who are on the road to getting type I diabetes (as shown in part by their having antibodies to islet cells, insulin, or GAD) but who have not yet arrived. Using insulin or drugs to suppress the immune system at this stage might stop T cells from killing the beta cells.

Researchers are giving people with a high risk of type I diabetes the immunosuppressant azathioprine or cyclosporine, or long-acting insulin, oral insulin, or nicotinic acid to see if these treatments can delay or prevent the development of the disease. Other experiments suggest that azathioprine can reduce the insulin dose needed in people who already have type I diabetes, if the drug is started at diagnosis.

As more is learned about the exact role of the autoantibodies in type I diabetes, other therapies may also become possible. For example, perhaps a drug might be tailored to seek out and destroy only those T cells that cause beta cell damage. Or, if autoimmunity to GAD turns out to be the primary cause, children might be immunized to prevent type I diabetes much as people today are immunized with flu or polio virus to prevent those diseases.

◆**Viruses**. Viruses, too, are a suspected trigger of type I diabetes. Often, people who develop type I diabetes have recently had a viral infection. Also, epidemics of type I diabetes sometimes occur after virus epidemics. In addition, several other autoimmune diseases are thought to be caused by viruses. Several viruses are associated with type I diabetes. These include not only the Coxsackie family of viruses but also the viruses that cause mumps and German measles.

Scientists are uncertain how viruses might bring

on type I diabetes. The theory that antibodies to Coxsackie B4 virus also attack GAD in beta cells explains only one of the many ways viruses may be involved. Another theory is that infection with the virus might change the structure of the molecules on the surface of islet cells. The changed antigen might then appear foreign to the immune system, stimulating an attack.

The eminent diabetes researcher Gian Franco Bottazzo believes type I diabetes is a relatively recent disease caused by a new slow-acting virus. Infection with this hypothetical virus causes the immune system to mount an immune attack against proteins in the pancreas. The spread of this new virus could explain the puzzling sudden and drastic increases in cases that occurred, for example, on the island of Sardinia in the 1960s and in Finland in the 1970s.

✦**Cold temperatures**. Type I diabetes is more common in countries with cold climates and develops more often in the winter than summer. Doctors are unsure what causes these associations but suspect that it could arise from virus epidemics, which are more common in winter.

✦**Cows' milk**. Strangely enough, rates of type I diabetes are higher in places where people drink lots of cows' milk. One study found that children newly diagnosed with type I diabetes had higher levels of antibodies to a specific protein in cows' milk than other children. These antibodies also act as autoantibodies, attacking a here-today, gone-tomorrow protein that sometimes appears on the surface of the insulin-producing beta cell after an illness. The researchers suggested that an infectious illness that resulted in production of that beta-cell protein would open an opportunity for the milk protein antibodies to attack the beta cells, perhaps starting the islet destruction that leads to type I diabetes. For the body to make antibodies to milk protein, they must leave the digestive system. This probably happens when cow's milk is given to babies younger than three months. An infant's digestive system is too young to stop the escape of whole proteins from the gut. Once the protein's outside the gut, the body makes antibodies to it. Add avoiding this problem to the list of good reasons to breastfeed.

✦**Oxygen free radicals**. Oxygen free radicals sound like a terrorist group, and in some ways, they are. These destructive molecules in the body don't care what they damage. They not only explode bacteria, but they also tear apart the body's own cells and damage their components. As a result, oxygen free radicals play a role in aging processes in the body and in the development of several diseases.

Many chemical reactions in the body produce oxygen free radicals as a by-product. Smoke, air pollution, and diet can sometimes cause additional production of free radicals. Although the body has ways to keep the free radicals under control, it is sometimes overwhelmed.

Some scientists suspect that oxygen free radicals play a role in type I diabetes. Islet cells are low in enzymes that break down free radicals. Thus, if something were to increase the number of these destructive molecules in the pancreas, they could run rampant. Oxygen free radicals may also contribute to some complications of diabetes. If this theory is right, then it may be possible to prevent diabetes with drugs that destroy or block the formation of free radicals in the islet cells.

✦**Chemicals and drugs**. The rat killer pyriminil (Vacor) can lead to the development of type I diabetes. Other chemicals can make animals diabetic, but it is unclear whether they have the same effect on humans. Two prescription drugs are also known to sometimes cause type I diabetes: pentamidine, a treatment for a kind of pneumonia, and L-asparaginase, an anticancer drug.

◆**Young age**. Puberty is the most common time for developing type I diabetes, and at least half of all people are diagnosed before age 30. The greater susceptibility of young people is unexplained.

Taking all these associations together, it seems that a person who develops type I diabetes starts with a genetic susceptibility and then has the misfortune to encounter a food or virus or some other factor that triggers the start of the disease. Thus, no one is predestined to get type I diabetes, but a person's own unique genetic and biochemical makeup can greatly increase the odds.

Diabetes Worldwide

Both genetic and environmental factors play a role in the development of diabetes. As a result, the number of people with diabetes varies among races and among countries. Even within the United States, cities vary dramatically in the rate of diabetes among their citizens. In fact, where a person lives is one of the most important influences of whether he or she gets type I diabetes. For example, the colder the climate, the greater the percentage of people with type I diabetes there usually are.

Following are some statistics on how many people get type I diabetes and who they are.

◆An estimated almost 14 million people in the United States have diabetes. Only about 700,000 of these people have type I diabetes. The rest have type II diabetes.

◆Of the nearly 14 million Americans who have type II diabetes, 50% have not yet been diagnosed. Sometimes the symptoms of type II diabetes are

subtle and can be attributed mistakenly to growing older.
✦Almost everyone whose diabetes is diagnosed before the age of 30 has type I diabetes.
✦Each year, about 13,000 people 19 years of age or younger are diagnosed with type I diabetes in the United States. (about 18 per 100,000 people in this age-group). For people older than 20, this figure is about 16,500 per year (about 9 per 100,000 people in this age-group).
✦White people are more likely to get type I diabetes than are black people, Hispanics, American Indians or Asians.
✦In high risk countries, boys seem a little more likely than girls to get type I diabetes.
✦The risk of developing type I diabetes by age 50 is about 1%.
✦The risk of developing type I diabetes is highest between the ages of 11 and 14.
✦Although the risk of getting type I diabetes drops greatly after puberty, even elderly people sometimes develop type I diabetes.
✦The risk of a child developing type I diabetes is higher than the risk of developing cancer, muscular dystrophy, juvenile rheumatoid arthritis, multiple sclerosis, or cystic fibrosis.
✦Scandinavian countries have the highest incidence (proportion of children developing the disease each year) of type I diabetes in the world, as many as 30 new cases per 100,000 children per year.
✦Asian and African countries are believed to have the lowest incidence of type I diabetes. The incidence in Japan is only 2 children per 100,000 each year.
✦The incidence of type I diabetes is increasing in Europe, Asia, and the Western Pacific.

How to Cure Diabetes

....

Only one way is now known to cure type I diabetes: give the body an internal source of insulin that can respond to high blood glucose levels.

Pancreas Transplantation

Surgeons accomplish this task by pancreas transplantation. During this operation, part or all of a pancreas is surgically placed within the abdomen of a person with type I diabetes. (The old pancreas is left in place because it still makes digestive enzymes.) A living relative who does not have diabetes may be able to donate half a pancreas, or a whole pancreas may come from a stranger who died but donated his or her organs to science.

When successful, a pancreas transplantation has almost miraculous effects. Recipients of transplants have normal glucose levels and no longer need to take insulin. Also, the progression of some of the side effects of diabetes can be stopped or even reversed. For example, people who had nerve damage due to diabetes before the transplant will probably get no worse and may gradually improve. Mild kidney disease caused by diabetes will also not get any worse. The effects of pancreas transplantation on diabetic eye disease are less clear-cut. Although eye disease continues to get worse at the same rate as before the operation, it may eventually stabilize.

However, pancreas transplantation has a grim side, too, making it inappropriate now for most people with type I diabetes. The worst problem is that the body treats the new pancreas as "foreign" and launches an immunologic attack on it. To prevent this, doctors start giving the patient drugs that control the immune system even before the operation. After the transplant is in place, the person must take these immunosuppressants, usually a combination of cyclosporine and azathioprine, for the rest of his or her life.

Unfortunately, immunosuppressive drugs reduce the person's resistance to infection and cancer, can cause kidney damage, pancreas damage, and disable the body's response to insulin. And despite the drugs, some or all of the new pancreas can be rejected, making insulin injections necessary.

Another problem with pancreas transplantation is that the surgery itself is very hard on someone who has an illness that affects most of the body, as diabetes does. About 15% of pancreas transplant recipients die within 5 years. Also, pancreas transplantation costs tens of thousands of dollars, far more than insulin therapy.

Because of the dangers of the surgery and immunosuppressant drugs, doctors usually recommend that people with type I diabetes receive a pancreas transplant only if they are also having (or already had) a kidney transplant. Because a kidney-transplant recipient needs to take immunosuppressants anyway, the pancreas transplant adds little extra risk and offers huge benefits. Some pancreas transplants have also been performed on people whose diabetes created problems more serious than the immunosuppressants were likely to cause.

Islet Transplantation
Another approach to curing diabetes, still in an experimental stage, is transplanting just the islet cells of the pancreas. They are the portion of the pancreas that secretes insulin. They also function to sense changes in blood glucose level, and react accordingly. For instance, when blood glucose levels drop, they stop releasing insulin.

In theory, transplanting only islet cells should

also cure diabetes. This approach would be much less dangerous than transplanting a whole pancreas and thus could occur shortly after diagnosis of type I diabetes, restoring normal glucose levels right away. Scientists have learned how to separate the islets from the other cells in a pancreas. But it is still unclear how many islet cells need to be transplanted to be effective or where in the body they should be placed. And the biggest problem, as with pancreas transplants, is rejection by the immune system. Finding new immunosuppressant drugs with fewer harmful effects on the body would be very helpful for both types of transplants. However, another option is available for islet cells—changing the cells themselves before transplanting them to fool the immune system into ignoring them.

The immune system is complex in some ways, but simple in others. A long chain of events must occur before the thymus can produce T cells, the immune system's soldiers specialized to attack something alien—a virus, bacterium, fungus, or a transplanted organ. (The thymus is a small organ located high in the chest.) Yet, each T cell has only one enemy, which it finds by simple means. If a molecule on the T cell fits like a jigsaw puzzle piece with a molecule (called an antigen) on another cell, the T cell can join that cell and destroy it. Imagine finding your car in a shopping mall parking lot by trying your key in the door of every car until you find a lock it fits. So, too, in looking for enemies, the T cell ignores every aspect of a cell except whether it carries an antigen that the T cell can bind to.

Researchers are trying to help transplanted islet cells avoid detection by T cells. One method is to cover the recognition site on each islet with a protein so that the T cell cannot bind to it. Some scientists are treating the cells with cold or ultraviolet light to change the shape of the recognition site, again stopping the T cell from binding to it. Another method is to transplant the islet cells into the thymus itself. Because T cells "learn" to recognize the body's own cells while still in the thymus, islet cells transplanted there are not seen as invaders by T cells. Yet another idea is to surround the transplanted islets with a special membrane that lets glucose and insulin out but does not let T cells in.

Even if the problem of rejection is worked out, another problem remains. This problem, shared by both pancreas and islet cell transplantation, is a shortage of organ donors. Of the people who die each year, very few do so under circumstances suitable for saving and transplanting their organs. And not all of these people have signed organ-donor cards or have relatives willing to give permission for the organs to be transplanted. At most, there are only 7,000 to 9,000 cadaver donors per year in the United States—far too few to supply pancreas or islet cells to everyone with type I diabetes. Some scientists believe the answer to the organ shortage lies in using organs from other species or from fetuses, but research in these areas is only beginning.

Two

All About Insulin

For thousands of years, people have asked what causes diabetes. Yet it has been only in the last century that the clues began to be uncovered. Luckily, you are able to benefit from these recent findings. And diabetes care is likely to get better—much better—in your lifetime.

We don't know how long humans have had diabetes. One of the earliest medical texts is called the Ebers Papyrus, dating from 1550 B.C. This ancient Egyptian document describes a condition of "passing too much urine," a problem that gives diabetes its name. Diabetes is a Greek word that means "pass through" or "siphon." In the second century A.D., the Greek physician Aretaeus chose the name because his patients' bodies appeared to "melt down" into urine. People also observed that the urine was sweet. One way to diagnose diabetes in early times was to pour urine near an anthill. If the urine attracted ants, that confirmed it had sugar. In the eighteenth century, the Latin term *mellitus* was added to describe this sugary taste.

Role of the Pancreas

There were many steps along the way to discovering what caused diabetes. Many seem obvious now but were only confirmed rather recently. It wasn't until 1776 that chemical tests proved the sugar glucose was in the blood of diabetic and nondiabetic people. At the time, scientists proposed that people with diabetes pass sugar from the blood to the urine. But how?

No one knew until 1889. German physiologists Oskar Minkowski and Joseph von Mering learned, somewhat by accident, that the pancreas was the key organ involved with diabetes. They were studying digestion of fat and decided to remove the pancreas of a laboratory dog. To their surprise, the dog urinated again and again. They had the presence of mind to test the urine for glucose. The dog had developed diabetes once it lost its pancreas.

Isolating Insulin

Now scientists could focus on finding what substance the pancreas secreted to prevent diabetes. The earliest substances isolated did not work well. Baffled by these failures, there was not much progress for another 30 years. Meanwhile, people with diabetes were subjected to a variety of so-called cures—bloodletting, opium, and special diets—that did little to help. Although special, almost starvation, diets seemed to help some older people with diabetes, they could not help the severely ill young patient. These young patients usually died within a year of developing diabetes.

In the spring of 1921, Dr. Frederick Banting, an inexperienced surgeon not long out of medical school, had an idea for an experiment to isolate the islets of Langerhans in the pancreas. Although Banting could not get any funding for his work, Professor J.J.R Macleod, an expert in carbohydrate metabolism at the University of Toronto, allowed

Banting to use his laboratory while he was on vacation. Macleod teamed Banting up with a young medical student named Charles Best.

Banting's idea was to tie off the pancreatic duct of some dogs. He felt this would destroy most of the pancreas because it would no longer be able to secrete its digestive enzymes into the intestine. However, he thought the islets of Langerhans, which secrete something directly into the blood, would survive. Next, Banting proposed to isolate a substance from these surviving cells and inject it into a diabetic dog. After many setbacks and many hours of intense work, Banting and Best finally succeeded in treating a diabetic dog with the extract from the islets.

About 6 months after their success with the diabetic dog, Banting and Best prepared an extract that was injected into Leonard Thompson, a 14-year-old boy who was dying of diabetes. The boy's condition did not improve. J.B. Collip, a biochemist in Macleod's laboratory, improved the extract by purifying it. The next trial on Leonard Thompson, 12 days later, was a success. Soon the young boy, whose body had wasted away leaving him looking almost like a skeleton, filled out. He lived for 15 more years, until he died from pneumonia.

In 1923, in one of the fastest recognitions of a medical discovery, Banting and Macleod were awarded the Nobel Prize in Physiology and Medicine for the discovery of insulin. The award sparked controversy. Banting immediately announced that he felt Best merited the award too, and he would share his prize money equally with Best. Similarly, Macleod shared his prize with Collip. Little did they know that the discovery of insulin was of such importance that there was room for everyone to be recognized.

Making Insulin Available

It was one thing to produce a small amount of extract from the pancreases of dogs and slaughterhouse animals. It was quite another to produce enough insulin for all the people with diabetes. The Toronto researchers granted Eli Lilly and Company of Indianapolis, Indiana, a 1-year license to produce enough insulin. Lilly succeeded in producing large quantities of purified insulin within a few months. By the end of 1923, insulin was available for treating people in the United States, Canada, and Europe. However, even as late as the 1930s, many doctors did not believe in prescribing insulin. It would take many years for doctors to become educated about what insulin was and how it worked.

Types of Insulin

There are many different insulin preparations available today. Table 1 lists them, along with their manufacturer, strength, and source. Although insulins from animal sources are highly purified, synthetic human insulin is less likely to cause an immune reaction. Your body's immune system goes into action when anything "foreign" enters. Naturally, human insulin looks less foreign to your body than insulin from a pig or cow. Pork insulin seems to cause fewer problems than beef or beef-pork mixtures.

When insulin was discovered in 1922, it was called "life in a bottle." It still is. But manufactured insulin has changed over time. In the early years, only rapid-acting insulin (Regular) was available. It was made from the pancreases of pigs and cows. People injected their Regular insulin before each meal and at bedtime (much like people on multiple injections do today). Unfortunately, the purity and strength of that insulin were not always reliable.

Table 1. Insulins

Product	Manufacturer	Form	Strength
Rapid acting (onset 1/2–4 hr)			
Humulin R (Regular)	Lilly	Human	U-100
Iletin I Regular	Lilly	Beef/Pork	U-100
Iletin II Regular	Lilly	Pork	U-100
Novolin R (Regular)	NovoNordisk	Human	U-100
Novolin R Penfill (Regular)	NovoNordisk	Human	U-100
Purified Pork R (Regular)	NovoNordisk	Pork	U-100
Regular	NovoNordisk	Pork	U-100
Velosulin Human (Regular)			
Buffered	NovoNordisk	Human	U-100
Intermediate acting (onset 2–4hr)			
Humulin L (Lente)	Lilly	Human	U-100
Humulin N (NPH)	Lilly	Human	U-100
Iletin I Lente	Lilly	Beef/Pork	U-100
Iletin I NPH	Lilly	Beef/Pork	U-100
Iletin II Lente	Lilly	Pork	U-100
Iletin II NPH	Lilly	Pork	U-100
Lente	NovoNordisk	Beef	U-100
Novolin L (Lente)	NovoNordisk	Beef	U-100
Novolin N (NPH)	NovoNordisk	Human	U-100
Novolin N Penfill (NPH)	NovoNordisk	Human	U-100
NPH	NovoNordisk	Beef	U-100
Purified Pork Lente	NovoNordisk	Pork	U-100
Purified Pork N (NPH)	NovoNordisk	Pork	U-100
Long acting (onset 4–6 hr)			
Humulin U (Ultralente)	Lilly	Human	U-100
Ultralente	NovoNordisk	Beef	U-100
Mixtures			
Humulin 50/50	Lilly	Human	U-100
(50% NPH, 50% Regular)			
Humulin 70/30	Lilly	Human	U-100
(70% NPH, 30% Regular)			
Novolin 70/30	NovoNordisk	Human	U-100
(70% NPH, 30% Regular)			
Novolin 70/30 Penfill	NovoNordisk	Human	U-100
(70% NPH, 30% Regular)			
Novolin 70/30 Prefilled	NovoNordisk	Human	U-100
(70% NPH, 30% Regular)			

Today, the action of all types of insulin, both Regular and delayed-action, is more predictable. This gives you more confidence in interpreting how diet and physical activity affect your blood glucose level.

Human Versus Pork or Beef Insulin

Insulin from each of these sources—whether human, pork, or beef—is effective in controlling blood glucose. However, human insulin is associated with the fewest side effects. If you are still using animal insulin and think you might want to give human insulin a try, raise this issue with your doctor. Never change your type of insulin without consulting your doctor. If you were diagnosed in recent years, you're probably already using human insulin.

Pork or beef insulin is isolated from the pancreases of pigs and cows that otherwise provide meat for people to eat. Pork insulin causes fewer allergic reactions in humans than beef insulin because pork insulin is almost identical to human insulin. It differs by just one amino acid (the building blocks of proteins, like insulin).

Recombinant human insulin is made possible through genetic engineering techniques. The human genetic code for insulin is inserted into bacteria, fooling the bacteria into producing human insulin. Because bacteria multiply rapidly, they can produce large amounts of insulin. This technology allows us an almost unlimited supply of insulin to meet the growing demands.

There are a few instances when you might consider using human insulin, for example, if you are

◆allergic to animal insulins;

◆pregnant or thinking about becoming pregnant;

◆developing dents or lumps under the skin at injection sites;

✦finding your injection sites red and swollen;

✦developing resistance to insulin (the same amount and type of insulin stops working as well as it used to);

✦using insulin only temporarily; or

✦opposed to using animal products based on your religious or ethical beliefs.

Share this information with your health-care team.

Action Times

Three characteristics of insulin are important to keep in mind when choosing the right insulin for you. They are:

✦**Onset**. The length of time before insulin reaches the bloodstream and begins lowering blood glucose.

✦**Peak time**. The time during which insulin is at its maximum strength in terms of lowering blood glucose levels.

✦**Duration**. This is how long the insulin continues to lower the blood glucose level.

Remember, each person has his or her unique response to insulin, so the times mentioned in Table 2 are approximate. Only blood glucose testing will tell how your body responds.

Regular insulin from pigs and cows was the first type of insulin widely available. Because it is short-acting, Regular insulin is given in multiple injections over the day. In 1946, the Danish researcher Hans C. Hagedorn developed NPH (Neutral Protamine Hagedorn), an intermediate-acting insulin. This insulin has a slower onset and lasts longer in the body. This slower action is beneficial because it can allow fewer injections per day. For example, an injection of NPH taken with Regular at breakfast can cover lunch and, thus, eliminate the need for another injection of Regular at lunch. Because some people were allergic to the protamine in NPH, another intermediate-acting insulin, Lente, was developed. An even longer-acting insulin, Ultralente, provides a continuous level of insulin release and has little if any peak effect. Human insulin usually has a faster onset and shorter duration than animal insulin (Table 2). This may be desirable or undesirable depending on the insulin injection schedule you have. Also note that human Ultralente might be considered an intermediate- rather than a long-acting insulin in some people. Whenever your doctor advises you to change insulin, you will have to find out the speed of action of the new insulin in your body.

Premixed Insulins
Often people will be instructed to take a given amount of Regular and a given amount of NPH in one injection. You can mix them yourself. See the instructions for mixing on page 242 of the Appendix.

Table 2. Insulins by Relative Action Times

Insulin Type	Onset (hours)	Peak (hours)	Usual Effective Duration (hours)	Usual Maximum Duration (hours)
Short-acting				
Human Regular	0.5–1.0	2–3	3–6	4–6
Animal Regular	0.5–2.0	3–4	4–6	6–8
Intermediate				
Human NPH	2–4	4–10	10–16	14–18
Animal NPH	4–6	8–14	16–20	20–24
Human Lente	3–4	4–12	12–18	16–20
Animal Lente	4–6	8–14	16–20	20–24
Long-acting				
Human Ultralente	6–10	—	18–20	20–30
Animal Ultralente	8–14	Minimal	24–36	24–36

Or you can buy insulin already mixed in certain combinations for the convenience (50/50 or 70/30 mixtures of NPH plus Regular insulins). Never mix types of insulin except as directed by your doctor.

There can be problems if you mix Regular with Lente or Ultralente insulin. These longer-acting insulins blend with the Regular, leading to unpredictable results in the absorption of the fast-acting insulin. If your injection program calls for both Lente and Regular at the same time, be advised to inject them immediately after mixing. Even with this precaution, many doctors have stopped prescribing a mixed Regular-Lente dose. If you don't get the response you expect from the Regular insulin, ask your doctor if you should increase the amount of Regular in the mix.

Insulin Strength

As long as you are buying insulin in this country, you do not have to worry about different strengths of insulin. The basic strength available in the United States is U-100. This means it has 100 units of insulin per milliliter of fluid. U-40, a weaker strength insulin, has been phased out, and U-500 is only available by special order for those who develop insulin resistance and require extremely high doses of insulin.

Insulin syringes also come in different sizes to match the strength of insulin. If you travel outside of the United States, bring along sufficient insulin and matching U-100 syringes. If you don't match insulin strength with the proper syringe, you can end up taking the wrong dose. If you plan a long stay out of the country and cannot bring all the supplies you need, remember that the U-40 insulin found in Latin America and Europe will require a U-40 syringe. Your doctor can help you adjust your dosage.

Additives

All insulins have added ingredients. These prevent bacteria from growing and help keep them from spoiling. Intermediate- and long-acting insulins also contain ingredients that prolong their action times. Sometimes these additives, such as the protamine in NPH, can cause allergic reactions.

Buying and Storing Insulin

It pays to shop around. Prices for insulin may vary by several dollars per bottle. You may receive a discount for buying certain quantities at your pharmacy or by mail order. Many insurance companies now have relationships with "preferred pharmacies" that offer insulin at reduced rates. Check with your insurance company to see if they have this service. These approaches can help keep your expenses down. When buying insulin (especially if you are buying in bulk), check the expiration date. You want to make sure you will use all the insulin before then.

Develop a relationship with a professional pharmacist. Feel free to ask questions. Don't just ask for "NPH insulin." Look at the full brand name, strength, and kind. Bring along an empty bottle to make sure you get exactly the same thing each time. Before you pay, double check to see that you have what you want. If you consistently use the same pharmacist, he or she will be able to contact you more easily if there is ever any problem that requires a batch of insulin to be recalled.

Consider choosing a pharmacy that is close by or one that delivers your insulin to you. Many people find they like the convenience of having their insulin delivered, especially if they are busy or ill.

You should store any insulin bottles you're not using in the refrigerator whenever possible. If you go through a bottle of insulin in about a month, you don't need to refrigerate it in between injections. Besides, injecting cold insulin can make the injection feel more painful. Put a cold bottle of insulin in your pocket for a few minutes to warm it up before you draw out the insulin, or warm a filled syringe by gently rolling it between your hands. If you store insulin in a cooler when on a trip, make sure the bottle doesn't come in contact with ice or freeze. Insulin spoils if it gets colder than 36°F. Don't expose your insulin to extremes of heat or even to prolonged sunlight. Insulin spoils if it gets hotter than 86°F. The general rule of thumb is, if the temperature is comfortable for you, your insulin will be okay, too.

Don't keep an open vial of insulin at room temperature for longer than about a month after you first puncture it. Otherwise, you risk contamination as well as decreased insulin strength. If you go through bottles slowly, it may help to write the date you first use a new bottle on the label. In some cases, manufacturers recommend that insulin not be used for longer than 7 days. For example, cartridges of Novo-Nordisk's 70/30 insulin mixture and Novolin N have this short life span once opened. For the sake of safety, check the instructions from your manufacturer.

Normal Appearance

Never use insulin that looks abnormal. Regular insulin is a clear liquid. Phosphate-buffered Regular is the preferred type of insulin for use in insulin pumps because this clear liquid helps prevent the pump from clogging. If you use Regular, check for particles or discoloration in the insulin. Any cloudiness may indicate contamination.

Other types of insulin are suspensions. That means there is solid material floating in liquid. It should look uniformly cloudy. However, if you use

NPH or Lente, look for and avoid any insulin that has "frosting" inside the bottle or large clumps floating in it. These changes in the insulin mean crystals are forming. This deterioration can be caused by excessive shaking of the insulin, extremes of temperature, and improper zinc/insulin ratios.

If you find any of these things wrong with your insulin at the time of your purchase, return it immediately. If the condition develops later, try to determine if you have stored or handled the insulin the wrong way. If not, talk to your pharmacist about a refund or exchange.

Insulin Delivery

Most people with diabetes use the standard needle and syringe method to get insulin into their bodies. This should be a quick, relatively painless self-care task. But if you have difficulty with any part of your insulin-injection routine, your doctor or diabetes educator can help you. Traditional insulin delivery by syringe is just one method, and there are aids to help if vision impairment or using your hands is causing you problems. More advanced delivery systems such as an insulin pump are a good choice for some people. No matter what method you choose, the basic purpose is the same: to deliver insulin into the fat just under your skin.

In the future, we may see alternative methods of insulin delivery more widely available. One exciting prospect is an implantable insulin infusion device. This may only need to be refilled every 2 months. And hopefully someday, there will be one sophisticated enough to sense your blood glucose level and even adjust your insulin level by itself.

Needles and Syringes

Today you can find needles that are slimmer, have sharper points, and are specially coated to slide into the skin smoothly. These improvements help make your injections practically painless. Disposable syringes with lubricated microfine needles will give the smoothest penetration of your skin and will be the least painful. If your injections are still painful, review your injection technique with your doctor or nurse educator. Learn to relax before you inject yourself. Tense muscles can make the injection hurt.

Keep your risk of infection low by making sure your injection site is clean. However, this does not mean you have to use alcohol to clean your injection site first. Some people even inject through hosiery or suit pants for convenience. See the Appendix, pages 241–46, for additional tips on preparing an insulin injection and reusing your syringe and needle.

Buying syringes. You must match your syringe to your insulin. This is not a big problem in the United States. Almost all insulin is U-100, so you need U-100 syringes. Your other consideration is syringe size. Your syringe needs to be large enough to hold your entire dose. For example, you'd have to inject two times to take a 45-unit dose with a 30-unit syringe. A 50-unit syringe would be better. (1cc=100 units, each line is 2 units. 1/2cc=50 units, each line is 1 unit. 1/3cc=30 units, each line is 1 unit.) Can you read the markings on the syringe? You need to do this to get an accurate dose. Perhaps a syringe with a different color plunger would make it easier for you to tell when the syringe is filled to the right level.

If you plan to be away from home, take along a doctor's prescription for syringes and perhaps a letter from him or her stating that you have diabetes and your insulin type. In some states, you may not be able to obtain your supplies, by law, without a prescription. If you encounter problems getting your supplies while traveling, try a hospital emergency room. (For more on traveling, see pages 191–93, Chapter 11.)

Reusing syringes. Deciding whether to use your syringe more than once is up to you. It's definately a money saver, and there's no evidence that reusing a properly maintained syringe increases your chance of infection. However, if you have poor personal hygiene, are ill, have open wounds on your hands, or have decreased resistance to infection for any reason, you should not risk syringe reuse. If a needle touches anything other than clean skin, it might carry germs into your body, and it's time to throw it away.

Getting rid of syringes. It's a very bad idea to toss an old syringe into the trash can. Used syringes are medical waste and need proper disposal. Your town or county may have rules about disposing of needles and other medical waste such as lancets. An accidental stick with your insulin syringe could give a stranger lots of worry.

Removing the needle will prevent anyone from ever using the syringe again. Clipping needles off syringes is a first step only if you do it correctly. It's best to buy a device that clips, catches, and contains the needle. Do not use scissors to clip off needle tips—the flying needle could hurt someone or become temporaily lost until someone is accidentally stuck with it. Bending your needle is another way to destroy it, if you can do it safely. One way is to pull out the plunger, push the needle into the plunger, bend the needle, break it off, and reinsert the plunger with the needle into the syringe. If you don't destroy your needles, recap them if you can do it safely. Place the needle or entire syringe in an opaque (not clear) heavy duty plastic or metal container with a screw cap or other closure. You don't want the syringes to escape once you've sent them to the dump. Do not use a container that will allow a needle to break through and possibly stick someone.

Insulin Pumps

Insulin pumps are miniature, computerized pumps, about the size of a call-beeper, that you can wear on your belt or in your pocket. They deliver a steady, measured dose of insulin through a flexible plastic tube with a small needle that is inserted through the skin into the fatty tissue and taped in place. On your command, the pump releases a bolus (a surge) of insulin; this is usually done just before eating to counter the rise in blood glucose.

Maybe you have thought about an insulin pump, but its cost, the inconvenience of being joined to a machine, or just thinking about making such a major change in your diabetes-care routine outweighed any benefits. It may be time for a second look. Pumps are comfortable. They weigh less than 4 ounces. The initial cost of the pump is substantial—$3,000 to $5,000—but with a doctor's prescription, some insurance companies will cover their use. You may be surprised to find out that you can take it off for about an hour or two from time to time and still maintain control.

The pump is a little marvel of technology:
- ✦It beeps if clogged,
- ✦It lets you know if the batteries run low,
- ✦It has dosage limits to stop an accidental overdose, and
- ✦It is programmable to let you change your baseline infusion of insulin to match your metabolism.

How it works. The pump provides a steady (basal) rate of insulin that trickles in at a slow rate, day and night. The basal rate for pumps can be adjusted from 0.1 to 10.0 units per hour. Before eating, you push a button to program in the size of the extra premeal portion of insulin, called a *bolus*. The size of the bolus is related to the grams of carbohydrate in your meal and your blood glucose level. Delivering a bolus of insulin is just like adjusting your premeal shot on a multiple injection routine—without the shot! Usually, you do not need to take an extra bolus with snacks unless the snack is large.

If you use a pump, you'll probably learn to estimate the number of carbohydrates in a meal. The ease of giving pump boluses allows you to have flexible insulin coverage for meals and snacks. You'll have to invest a lot of time at the beginning to find the best basal rates, to find out when to adjust that basal rate, and to find how big a bolus you need per meal. This may help you even out your blood glucose levels and lead to a more flexible eating schedule. Remember that a pump does not sense your body's need for insulin and adjust by itself. You still need to take multiple blood glucose readings daily.

Many people choose the abdomen for pump insulin delivery. This area is convenient to use and gives a reliable, uniform absorption of insulin. How you insert the insulin needle varies between brands. Some are easier to remove temporarily because you can leave the infusion set in place, then just reattach the pump. With the Sof-set product, the needle is removed and the soft Teflon catheter remains in place. You don't have to worry that it will hurt when you exercise or if someone bumps into it. Every 1–3 days the infusion set needs to be moved to a new site.

The major problems of using a pump are in insulin delivery. Clogged or kinked tubing may reduce insulin delivery, although alarms warn you when this is happening. An infection or inflammation at the insertion site can also cause delayed insulin absorption. Less commonly, the metal needle may cause a reaction in the surrounding skin. Overuse of an infusion site can cause the same skin problems that failing to rotate your needle and syringe injection sites does (see below). Scarring can occur.

It is important to inspect the delivery site each day to make sure there is no insulin leakage or infection.

Advantages. A major advantage of a pump is that you don't have to stop what you're doing and fill a syringe. You just push a button to give yourself your insulin before meals. You can do this anywhere, anytime.

Pumps are also precise. You can set them to put out as little as one-tenth of a unit (0.1 unit) of insulin per hour. The insulin is pumped from a filled syringe through a thin plastic tubing to a needle or catheter inserted under the skin. Depending on the size of the syringe, the pump can hold a 1- or 2-day supply of insulin. The tubing varies in length, but it is long enough to allow plenty of slack for normal body movement.

Who should use a pump? Having trouble sticking to your current testing and injection routine? Then a more intense practice such as multiple daily injections or an insulin pump may not be for you. However, the potential benefits may motivate you to a new level of commitment.

Often the people best suited to a pump are those who have an urgent or special need to get tight control and gain flexibility. Maybe you're pregnant and want the best control possible. Maybe your job requires odd work hours, and it's hard enough to balance work, family, and meals during the week without having to adjust to new schedules every weekend. Maybe you have had unwanted swings in blood glucose while using intermediate- or long-acting insulin, and you are anxious to get your glucose levels in check. People who want an insulin plan that adapts to day-to-day changes in their lifestyle might like an insulin pump.

Choosing a pump. There are two continuous subcutaneous insulin infusion (CSII) pumps on the market today—the MiniMed and the Disetronic models. Your doctor or diabetes educator may have reasons to prefer one over the other. But your best bet for information may be to talk to a satisfied user of a pump. Here are a few things you'll want to know:

✦Is it waterproof? One style is waterproof, so you don't need to remove it when you shower or swim, although you may find it more convenient. The other is splashproof and has a waterproof pouch. Both must be removed if you want to dive into the pool, but you can shower or swim with either.

✦Can you adjust the basal (baseline) rate for different times of day? New pumps can alter the basal rate up to four times a day. For example, your basal rate is likely to be greater from 3 a.m to 7 a.m. than during the rest of the day.

✦Does the pump manufacturer offer a 24-hour 800 number so you can talk to service people toll free about problems? It can be a comfort to talk through your concerns and questions when you start something new.

✦How often will you have to change the pump's infusion site? The infusion is changed every 2 or 3 days.

✦How often do you need to change the batteries in the pump? Batteries last from 2 to 4 months.

✦What kind of insulin does the pump use? Usually, pumps use phosphate-buffered human Regular insulin, although phosphate-buffered pork insulin can be used too. Most pumps hold a 2-day supply of insulin. The phosphate-buffered solution helps keep the insulin flowing smoothly and keeps the pump from clogging.

✦How long can I take off the pump? Most people prefer to remove it during lovemaking. Some take it off to exercise. How long you can keep it off without a supplementary injection depends, in part, on how active you are when the pump is off. For example, a professional dancer might be able to keep it off for an entire performance because of the effect of exercise on blood glucose. You might need to inject some insulin while you're not wearing the pump. You will learn by experience and testing.

Injection Aids

Injection aids are devices that make giving an injection easier and those that don't require a needle and syringe. Many of these aids can help give you greater access to more injections sites in those hard to reach places. Talk with your doctor or diabetes educator about these products. Often, they can give you samples to try before you purchase any. Then you'll have a better idea if it is right for you. The ADA's annual *Buyer's Guide to Diabetes Supplies* lists information on different types of aids (see Resources, page 250).

Insertion aids. An automatic injector shoots a needle into your skin painlessly and almost without you knowing it. Some also automatically release the insulin when the needle enters the skin. With others, you have to press the plunger on the syringe. If you fear needles, this may be for you because you don't see the needle in advance. An automatic injector is helpful if you have arthritis or other problems holding a syringe steadily.

Infusers. These reduce the number of times you have to pierce your skin. With a special catheter needle, you insert an infusion tube into your abdomen. This remains in place at the injection site for two or three days. Insulin is injected into the tube that reseals after each needle entry. Because these infusers are usually sold in boxes of 4 or 10, ask your doctor whether you can try just one before you commit yourself to buying a whole box. There is an increased risk of infection with this aid, so you may have to learn how to keep your technique more sterile than usual.

Jet injectors. Want to be free of needles altogether? Maybe the jet injector is for you. The insulin is shot out so fast that it acts like a liquid needle, passing directly through the skin. This is another good choice for someone who fears or has trouble with needles. It also may be the right choice for someone who wants to increase the number of injections each day. Most injectors are easy enough for kids to use and load themselves.

Another advantage of the jet is that your insulin is less likely to pool under the skin. Instead, insulin spreads out and is absorbed more quickly. You may be able to give your shots closer to mealtime and not worry about waiting a half hour or so to eat. For some people, there is no difference in absorption compared with syringes.

A jet injector is expensive. Check with your insurance company about coverage of this aid. Over time you will save the cost of needles and syringes, but it is a large initial cost. Also, if you bruise easily, you may want to test an injector before you make this investment. Bruising is sometimes a problem, particularly with thin people, kids, and the elderly.

Another disadvantage of this device is the amount of time you must invest in taking it apart, sterilizing it by boiling, and reassembling it, about every 2 weeks. Germicidal cleaners, if you do not find them irritating, make cleaning easier because you do not have to take the injector apart. Still you may consider syringes a simpler option. Ask your doctor and diabetes educator what their patients think of jet injectors.

Pen injectors. An insulin pen looks just like an ink pen. It has a disposable needle instead of a writing point, and in place of an ink cartridge, there is an insulin cartridge. These pens are popular because they are so convenient and accurate in dose. You don't have to worry about filling syringes ahead of time and carrying them with you when you are away from home. Each pen cartridge holds 150 units of insulin that can be delivered in the measured amounts you need. You can find cartridges of Regular insulin, premixed 70/30 insulin, or NPH insulin.

You decide the number of units you want, stick the needle in your skin, and inject the insulin. The ability to adjust the dose makes them useful for multiple dose regimens.

Aids for the visually impaired. Several products are available to make injections easier for people who are visually impaired. They include:

✦Dose gauges to help you measure your insulin accurately (even mixed doses). Some have an audible click with each 1 to 2 units of insulin, and others have Braille or raised numbers.

✦Needle guides and vial stabilizers to help you insert the needle into the insulin vial correctly. A few of these also allow you to set a desired dosage level with a dial or other device.

✦Syringe magnifiers to enlarge the measure marks on an insulin syringe barrel. One model combines the magnifier with the needle guide and vial stabilizer and another clips around the syringe like a sleeve and magnifies the scale.

Be aware that some of these aids fit only specific brands of syringes. You may want to consider using some of these aids in combination with the devices already mentioned. In addition to these injection aids, you can find blood glucose monitors for the visually impaired. (See Chapter 5 Tools of the Trade.)

Injection-Site Rotation

Personal preference plays a big part in choosing where to inject your insulin. Perhaps it's easier to inject yourself in the abdomen than in the thigh. Perhaps not. The important thing is that you have choices. Wherever you choose to inject, you need to rotate the injection site within that body area to prevent problems in and under the skin. In general, your injection sites should be rotated within one general area, such as the abdomen, rather than switching randomly around the body. Once each injection site in that body area has been used, you can start over in the same body area. Moving on to another body area can cause differences in the rate at which you absorb the insulin.

Preferred Sites
Four areas of the body have enough tissue under the skin for insulin injection: the upper arm, the abdomen, the thighs, and the buttocks. Some people, particularly if you have a larger body size, have other options such as the lower back (as long as there is enough fat under the skin). When injecting, keep these basics in mind:

✦Divide the body area into quarter-sized injection sites. Guide yourself by making the injection at least a finger-width away from your last shot. (You'll need to find a way to remember where that last site was.)

✦Inject in the outer back part of the upper arms where there is fatty tissue. Steer clear of the deltoid muscle, the large triangular muscle that covers the shoulder joint. You should not inject into muscle.

✦Inject anywhere in the abdomen, but avoid a 2-inch space around the navel, which has tough tissue that causes erratic absorption. You may also find unpredictable insulin absorption when you inject too near to moles or scar tissue anywhere on the body.

✦Inject in the top and outside of the thighs. Avoid the inner thighs because rubbing between the legs may make the injection site sore. Watch out that you don't inject in the bony area above the knees where there isn't much fat.

Differences in Absorption

Research has shown that insulin is absorbed most quickly when it is injected into the abdomen, more slowly when injected in the arms, and slower still when injected in the thighs and buttocks. Many doctors recommend the abdomen. It may slow absorption of insulin, but it still goes at a consistent speed. After you have been injecting your abdomen for a week to ten days, you can imagine that your response to insulin would be different when you suddenly change to injecting your thigh. If you take insulin in one body area routinely, you probably know about how long it will take for it to go into effect, and you may have achieved good control using just that one area.

But suppose you still have swings in blood glucose that you can't explain, or your rotation pattern doesn't give you the results you expect. Some doctors are now recommending a different approach to site rotation that evens out those swings by taking into account the absorption rates from different areas of the body. Here's how it works.

Suppose you need a fast response from your insulin in the morning because you are a big breakfast eater, but want a slower response from your nighttime insulin because you like to go to bed early and need it to last through the night. Which sites would you choose based on absorption rates? In the morning, you would choose a site like the abdomen or even the arms. For the evening, the legs would be a better choice. Based on this knowledge of your needs, you would plan a systematic rotation plan in which you would inject the abdomen every morning and the leg every evening.

Other factors such as your diet, exercise, and stress level may make your responses the opposite of what you might expect just based on the absorption site. For example, strenuous exercise may cause your insulin to be absorbed more quickly than usual so that your blood glucose level isn't where you expect it to be. So what can you do? Routinely test your blood glucose. It is the only way to make sure the response you are having is the one you planned. Then you'll know if you have a site rotation plan that will work for you.

Injection Sites and Exercise

Research suggests that strenuous exercise of muscles near an injection site makes insulin act more rapidly than normal. This may be possible because of increased blood flow to the exercising muscles. There isn't enough evidence to recommend that you stop injecting in the areas of your body used in exercise. However, if you notice that your insulin is peaking faster when you exercise than you would expect, you may have to keep the idea of rapid absorption in mind. In any case, it's a good idea to avoid strenuous exercise during the peak action times of your insulin. Insulin plus exercise can lead to severe hypoglycemia.

Remember when you exercise you also have to decide whether you will eat more or take less insulin.

With experience, you will learn how to balance all of these things. Good blood glucose monitoring (SMBG) test data will help you figure out these ups and downs in blood glucose.

Skin Problems at Injection Sites

There are two main skin problems that occur at injection sites: *atrophy* and *hypertrophy*. With atrophy, tissue under the skin breaks down and results in dents in the skin. Hypertrophy is an overgrowth of extra cells, usually fat cells, that make the skin look lumpy. It can look similar to scar tissue. Site rotation is one way to avoid these problems. Another way is to make sure that your problems aren't caused by the type of insulin you're using.

Atrophy, also called *lipodystrophy*, probably is caused by your body's normal immune reaction toward an injected "foreign" substance. It is not common with human insulin. In addition to site rotation to prevent atrophy, it is important to use highly purified insulin, preferably human or pork. Young women seem to be more likely to get atrophy. If you find these depressions unsightly, ask your doctor about steroid or human insulin treatment. Human insulin is injected in the margins of the dented area as a way to build up fat and get rid of the depressions. This is not a quick fix, and it may take many months for improvement.

Hypertrophy does not appear to be an immune reaction. Thus, you do not have to change your type of insulin. However, you do need to change sites to get rid of this. By using the same sites over and over, you are encouraging fat deposits to accumulate in that area, called *lipohypertrophy*. You may be reluctant to change because injections seem less painful in these areas, and this may be true because the hypertrophy can numb the area. On the other hand, injections in these areas can also be more painful than usual. You should rotate your injection sites because the abnormal cell growth can limit the absorption of your insulin. Do not inject into the lumps; insulin action may be restricted by not being able to move through the tissue. Inject around the lumps.

Three

Glucose Balance: The Basics

Each day, your challenge is to keep your blood glucose at healthy levels. Food pushes glucose level up. Insulin brings it down. Stress drives it up. Exercise reduces it. How can you find the right balance among all these things? Everyone with diabetes reacts somewhat differently to each of these. There is no single prescribed path to follow. You must find your own way. Your doctor, nurse educator, dietitian, and other members of your health-care team can help you. Your ultimate goal is to have blood glucose levels as close to nondiabetic levels as possible *for you*. These levels are your ideal blood glucose levels.

The single most important thing you can do for yourself is to self-monitor your blood glucose. Unless you know how your body responds to food, insulin, activity, and stress, you can't make improvements. Trial and error, mixed with some patience, can help you achieve better control.

Your Changing Glucose Levels

Food
Your body breaks down the carbohydrate in food to glucose. The glucose travels through your blood to nourish every part of your body. Every

time you eat, your blood glucose levels will normally go up.

One take-charge tool is to learn on a day-to-day basis how food affects your blood glucose levels. Some of your body's reactions to food may even surprise you. Have you found that your blood glucose rises faster with carrots than sweet potatoes? Or faster with mashed potatoes than ice cream? As you learn how your body reacts, you can make appropriate adjustments so that your blood glucose will not rise too high, too quickly.

How you eat is a crucial part of your diabetes therapy. More and more Americans are taking a good look at what they are eating. You will have lots of company in eating a healthy diet. Your meal plan should help you pick foods in amounts matched by your insulin levels each time you eat. Until you learn your body's response to your insulin and to different foods, get the help of a dietitian in making this match. Insist on a meal plan that fits your tastes. Then you will be more likely to stick with it. (For more on meal planning and meal planning tools, see pages 151–60, Chapter 8.)

Insulin

As your body digests what you eat, glucose builds up in the blood unless your body has insulin ready to go to work. Insulin helps transport glucose from the blood into each cell of the body that needs it. Without insulin, cells suffer from lack of food. Because your body no longer makes insulin, you are in charge of supplying what you need.

The ideal treatment of type I diabetes would come close to matching the body's natural glucose-insulin response. In people without diabetes, glucose levels are close to the same most of the time. The body has a little bit of insulin ready to work at any time. For meals, it does a good job of releasing the right amount of extra insulin in time to clear glucose from the blood before glucose levels rise too high.

Ideally, you should eat meals and snacks during the time your insulin injection is having its greatest effect—while the insulin is active. If you eat too soon after an injection, your glucose can go too high. If you wait too long to eat after an injection, your blood glucose can drop too low. See Table 1 for guidelines on timing your premeal Regular insulin shot by your premeal blood glucose level. In most cases, you need to inject Regular insulin well before (30 to 45 minutes before) you eat so the insulin is ready when glucose enters the blood.

In addition to timing, you also need to match your food amount to insulin level. If you inject your usual dose of insulin and then eat more dinner than you had planned, what can happen? High blood glucose. On the other hand, if the meal isn't up to your expectations and you eat less, your blood glucose

Table 1. Timing Your Insulin Injection

If 45 minutes before meal, blood glucose is	Inject Regular insulin
Below 50 mg/dl*	When completing the meal
50-70 mg/dl*	At mealtime
70-120 mg/dl	15 minutes before eating
120-180 mg/dl	30 minutes before eating
Over 180 mg/dl	45 minutes before eating

*You need to eat right away—your blood glucose level is too low.

level will drop too low.

Even if you keep your food intake and activity exactly the same from day to day, there's something you won't be able to control: how your body takes in and uses the insulin you inject. How much insulin your body absorbs can change by as much as 25 % from day to day. This is especially true of NPH insulin. So, expect differences. You can discover them by testing your blood glucose and adjust for them by increasing or decreasing your next Regular insulin dose.

Exercise

Being physically active is a hot topic these days as people think more about health. Exercise not only makes you feel and look good, it improves your blood flow and muscle tone and even beats stress. Aerobic exercise—the kind that makes your heart work at a steady higher rate—gives your heart and lungs a particularly good workout. It increases the pumping power of the heart and gets blood flowing through your smallest blood vessels. This helps prevent the circulatory problems that people with diabetes can get. Walking is probably the best all-around exercise. It is something almost everyone can do.

During exercise, working muscles use their glucose stores for fuel. When the glucose begins to run low, glucose from the blood is used. In this way, exercise helps people with type I diabetes use up some blood glucose for energy. In addition, exercise seems to make muscles and other tissues more sensitive to insulin so less is needed to move glucose from the blood into the muscle cells. If you get regular exercise, you may be able to eat a little more or inject a little less insulin.

When you exercise, you have to be careful that your blood glucose levels do not drop too far, too fast. This happens most often in the hours after exercise, when your muscles are restoring glucose by taking it from the blood. Blood glucose levels can also drop while you exercise. On the other hand, if blood glucose levels are too high (over 250 mg/dl) while you exercise, activity may actually make your blood glucose level go up rather than down. (For more on exercise, see Chapter 9.)

Stress

Our lives seem more stressful today. People with diabetes often try to do more than everyone else, just to prove that diabetes isn't a disability. Be sensible. Everyone gets tired. Everyone needs time out to relax and recover from the stresses of everyday life. Remember stress can shoot your blood glucose out of your desired range and even contribute to ketoacidosis (diabetic coma). Stress is often a hidden contributor to swings in blood glucose. Perhaps it's because it is not as easily measured as grams of carbohydrate, units of insulin, or minutes of exercise. When you are not able to figure out why your blood glucose is so high, despite "doing everything right," think about your stress level.

Your Blood Glucose Goals

It is ideal to have glucose levels in the same range as a healthy person without diabetes (Table 2). For most people with type I diabetes, this just isn't realistic. You and your health-care team should decide together what goals are best for you. The goals need to be based on you: your needs, lifestyle, and health. You will be able to reach realistic goals. You will not be able to reach unrealistic ones, and setting, but not reaching, them will only hurt your self-confidence.

Write down all acceptable blood glucose range for

you at this time. The range could be something like 70 to 200 mg/dl. This means that under 70 mg/dl is too low and over 200 mg/dl is too high. This range will include relatively lower glucose levels for before meals, and somewhat higher glucose levels 1 or 2 hours after meals. Table 2 gives some sample ranges. As you gain greater glucose control, you'll see the high end of the ranges come down.

When you feel frustrated, remember that diabetes is a complicated disease. Because everyone responds a little differently to diet, exercise, and insulin, the answers to how much to eat, how much to exercise, and how much insulin to take are not always obvious. You may find a support group helpful in reaching toward your goals.

Self-Monitoring Schedule
How often should you test? Because you're the one who has to do it, only you can answer this question. Frequent testing can offer more choices. It lets you feel more in charge of what is going on with your body. Your doctor or diabetes educator can recommend a testing schedule, but it's really up to you, how often you're willing to test, and what supplies you can afford. Your insurance company may require

---

Table 2. Sample Blood Glucose Goals (mg/dl)

	Nondiabetic Level	Tight Control Goal	Your Goal May Be:
Fasting or before meals	Under 115	Under 120	120 to 140
Two hours after meals	Under 140	Under 180	180 to 220

a doctor's prescription before reimbursing you for the strips. They may refuse to cover them at all. You can request a periodic review of this policy.

Useful times for blood tests include before meals, before bed, and, on occasion, in the early morning (around 2 a.m. or 3 a.m.). You can use these results to make adjustments in your insulin dose or diet. You might consider doing early-morning tests if you have low blood glucose reactions overnight or wake up with very high blood glucose levels. It may also help you to know your blood glucose level 1 or 2 hours after you eat, to see the effects of various foods or combinations of foods.

Here are some instances when frequent blood glucose testing is recommended:

✦When changing your insulin injection plan, your diet, or exercise plan;

✦When you are sick;

✦When you are pregnant or considering becoming pregnant;

✦When you have trouble recognizing the warning signals of hypoglycemia;

✦When your levels have been dangerously high or low (outside your acceptable range);

✦When you start taking a medication that may affect blood glucose levels or your ability to recognize low blood glucose warning signs (ask your doctor or pharmacist about each prescription); and

✦When you are on intensive insulin therapy (see pages 79–80, Chapter 4).

There are times when self-monitoring of your blood glucose can clear up questions about how you feel. Are you sweating and feeling a little shaky because of your workout? Or are you having a low blood glucose reaction? A blood test will tell you for sure. Without the results, you may tend to eat because you fear your blood glucose level is low when it may really be too high.

Over time, you will gain confidence in your ability to manage your diabetes. You may think you can test less often. Be careful that you don't convince yourself that you can tell your blood glucose level by how you feel. Research shows that few people can guess their blood glucose level. Guessing is dangerous, particularly if your blood glucose level tends to fall with very little warning.

If you stop testing for a long period, ask yourself whether you're frustrated and trying to avoid facing problems in managing your diabetes. Monitoring can sometimes be depressing. You may get results that are way TOO HIGH for no apparent reason. The best thing to do is to talk with your doctor or nurse educator. They can help you track down the culprit. Perhaps you'll need a new approach to insulin therapy. Don't give up on testing.

Facing Your Results

When you are learning how to do self-monitoring, your first concern is doing the test correctly. If an unexpected reading shows up, check your technique and see whether the meter has a problem. Always keep your meter calibrated according to the manufacturer's instructions. When you get a new meter, learn how to take care of it (cleaning, glucose control solution, and how). You may want to ask your doctor or nurse educator to watch you test to check your method.

If you are faced with an unexpected high or low blood glucose reading and the meter is working fine, it's tempting to blame yourself. Maybe you know why your blood glucose is higher than you would like— the extra helping at dinner or failing to make it to your exercise class. Record your blood glucose honestly, and be glad you can figure out why it's the level it is so the next time you can make more appropriate adjustments.

Writing down your daily results in a record book helps you know your blood glucose patterns. Ask your doctor or nurse educator for a record book with an easy-to-use format, or make your own. Some blood glucose meters store 10, 20, or as many as 250 test results in their memory, saving you from having to write your results down each time, but you still need to see the patterns. Share your records with each member of your health-care team when you see them. This is the daily record that can explain your glycated hemoglobin levels (see below).

Your records can help you spot patterns in your blood glucose readings. Once you decide what the patterns mean, you can fine tune your insulin, food, or exercise. Your doctor or nurse educator can help you do this. For example, if you have high blood glucose levels in the morning, explore whether this is a result of too much food at bedtime, not enough insulin, or too much insulin with "rebounding" from a very low blood glucose level while you sleep. If you find a series of puzzling high or low results, talk with your doctor or nurse educator.

Insulin Plans

Once, Twice, or Many Times a Day?

How often should you inject insulin? There is no one right answer. But remember your purpose in taking insulin—making up for a malfunctioning pancreas. Well then, it makes sense to put insulin into your body as close to the way a normal pancreas would. A normal pancreas puts out a steady stream of insulin (a basal or baseline dose) day and night, and then secretes extra insulin in response to meals (a bolus).

How does your insulin regimen measure up to that standard? Would a new approach be better? Have a frank discussion with your health-care team. They will choose a plan with you. Once you've tried it out, maybe you can see where you need to alter it. Instead of always saying "Everything is just fine," speak up if anything is bothering you. Is there a problem when you exercise? Are you afraid to take a job that might require more travel? Are you more tired than you think you should be? Maybe it's time for a change. Unless you bring up the possibility of change or mention problems with your blood glucose test results, each member of your health-care team may assume you are satisfied with things as they are.

Changing your insulin plan requires time and energy to make sure you are solving problems, not creating new ones. But the end result should make you feel better and fit the life you want to live. If you are trying a new approach, here are some questions to ask:

✦How long will this type of insulin take to get into my bloodstream?

✦When will it be most active?

✦How long can I expect it to lower blood glucose?

✦How will my choice of injection site affect absorption?

✦Will choosing something other than a needle and syringe affect insulin absorption?

✦Can I mix different types of insulin in one shot without affecting their action?

✦How often and at what time of day should I inject my insulin?

Go step by step through this new insulin routine for a typical day with your doctor or nurse educator. Talk about how to adjust for an unusual day—oversleeping, illness, or travel. Write everything down. Compare what you expect with what actually happens to you.

Many things—your choice of insulin, blood glucose, food, exercise, and stress levels—can make a difference in how your body reacts. Human insulin, for example, has a slightly faster absorption rate and shorter duration than animal insulin. And if you have a high blood glucose level at injection time, your insulin has more work to do. Even things that you might not expect can affect the action of insulin. For example, injecting insulin after a warm shower can speed the insulin on its way because the warm water dilates the blood vessels just under your skin. The only way to know what each of these variables does to your blood glucose is to test. This will give you the best information on whether your insulin plan is right for you.

One Shot

One shot of insulin a day, only one needle a day—it sounds too good to be true. Unfortunately, it probably is. A single shot of intermediate-acting insulin only stays in your bloodstream for about 18 hours. Suppose you inject yourself when you get up at 7 a.m. What are your potential problems? Look at Graph 1 and note:

✦First, you will not have any insulin coverage until about 4 hours later, around 11 a.m. That may be fine for lunch, but what about breakfast?

✦Second, you are most vulnerable to hypoglycemia when the insulin peaks about 10 hours later, around 5 p.m. So it's time for dinner.

✦Finally, you have no coverage for much of the night because the insulin fades out after about 18 hours, and it's only 1 a.m.

In total, that leaves your glucose level unchecked for about 10 out of 24 hours in the day, from the time the insulin fades out at 1 a.m. until your next shot is

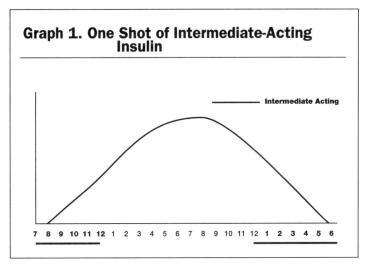

Graph 1. One Shot of Intermediate-Acting Insulin

————— Intermediate Acting

7 8 9 10 11 12 1 2 3 4 5 6 7 8 9 10 11 12 1 2 3 4 5 6

effective around 11 a.m. Graph 1 sketches out what may happen based on average absorption rates and action times of intermediate insulin. You can see how vulnerable you could be to having your blood glucose out of control. Lack of control puts you at higher risk for complications.

You must plan to have your major meals during the peak action time of the insulin. Can you always eat at the same time? Are your family and friends available to eat dinner during your peak time. This insulin plan, although convenient, is not very flexible and locks you into a more rigid lifestyle than is necessary.

Of course, there are exceptions. People who have some pancreatic function (during the honeymoon period) can do well on a one-shot-a-day routine. But otherwise, it is not advised. Its shortcomings can be seen in your blood glucose tests. Look at what percentage of your blood glucose readings are in the normal range, particularly during the periods before and after injection. Don't fool yourself by only taking your blood glucose readings at times when you "know" they will be all right.

More Than One Shot

Splitting your total intermediate-acting insulin dose into two shots (morning and evening) gives better coverage than a single shot (Graph 2). Generally, the morning shot will be a larger portion of the total daily dose than the evening shot. However, you can

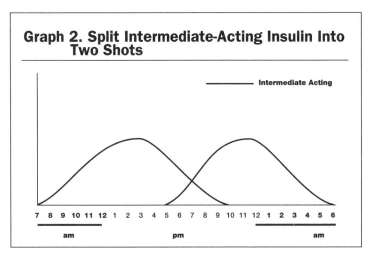

Graph 2. Split Intermediate-Acting Insulin Into Two Shots

improve your coverage more by not only splitting your insulin dose between two shots, but also mixing short- and intermediate-acting insulins in each dose (Graph 3).

Typically, this splitting and mixing approach would combine Regular and NPH insulins, generally taken about 30 minutes before breakfast and dinner. As the action of the short-acting insulin begins to wear off, the intermediate type kicks in. The ratio of intermediate- to short-acting is usually started at 2 to 1, until the proper balance can be reached. You can use a premixed formula (for example, 70/30 NPH/Regular), but you may want to split and mix the doses yourself. This allows you to change the amount

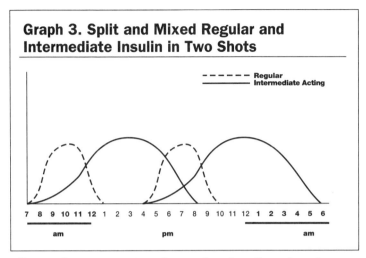

Graph 3. Split and Mixed Regular and Intermediate Insulin in Two Shots

- - - - - Regular
———— Intermediate Acting

7 8 9 10 11 12 1 2 3 4 5 6 7 8 9 10 11 12 1 2 3 4 5 6

am   pm   am

of Regular or NPH independently of each other as you want to account for your activity level and food intake.

Remember that Lente and Ultralente insulins must be injected right after mixing them with Regular or the action of the Regular insulin will be lessened. If you are not getting the rapid action you would expect from Regular, you may have to increase the amount of Regular you take. Alternatively, some people take the Lente (or Ultralente) and Regular in separate shots at the same time. Of course, this increases the total number of shots per day. There are two ways to have the best chances that this mixture will have about the same action each time: you can store the mixture for the same length of time before using it, so that the strength of the Regular insulin is lessened by about the same amount each time, or always take the shot right after mixing it. Unless you are already well-controlled on a program of mixing these types of insulin, it is not recommended that you start one.

When you are using a two-shot plan, you need—

at a minimum—premeal blood glucose readings to keep tabs on your body's response. A two-shot program gives you better control than a single shot but still keeps you closely tied to a regular meal schedule and a regular pattern of activity. This is because you cannot make short-term adjustments in longer-acting insulins. Only regular insulin can be immediately adjusted in direct response to a blood glucose test or schedule change.

If you find that you have low blood glucose in the early morning (2 a.m. or 3 a.m.) with the two-shot approach, think about using a three-shot program: a short- and intermediate-acting insulin mixture at breakfast, short-acting insulin at dinner, and intermediate-acting insulin at bedtime (Graph 4). Or if you have high blood glucose in the morning, you may need to move your shot from dinnertime to bedtime.

As the frequency of your insulin injections increases, you have more opportunities to fine-tune your control. The shots, to be most effective, must be accompanied by frequent blood glucose tests to make sure you have the desired effects.

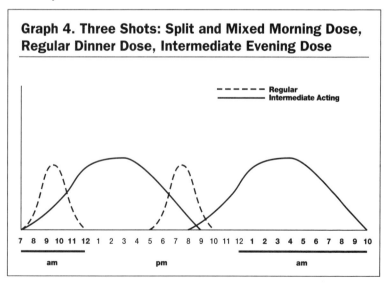

Graph 4. Three Shots: Split and Mixed Morning Dose, Regular Dinner Dose, Intermediate Evening Dose

- - - - - Regular
———— Intermediate Acting

7 8 9 10 11 12 1 2 3 4 5 6 7 8 9 10 11 12 1 2 3 4 5 6 7 8 9 10

am   pm   am

Intensive Insulin Therapy
When is increasing the intensity of insulin therapy the appropriate choice for you? Ask yourself:
◆Am I doing everything right yet still can't get control of my blood glucose?
◆Do my blood glucose tests frequently show unexpected levels, high or low?
◆Do I have signs of the complications of diabetes?
◆Do I lack the amount of energy I need to participate in all my activities—both day and night?
◆Do I want more flexibility in my lifestyle for timing meals, exercise, and other activities?
If you answer yes to any of these questions, you may want to investigate intensive insulin therapy more closely. See Chapter 4 Intensive Diabetes Treatment.

Too Little Insulin

Whatever your insulin routine, a rare and serious emergency can arise if you neglect high blood glucose. Diabetic ketoacidosis (DKA) can cause a coma, shock, pneumonia, breathing difficulties, and even death. Small children may experience swelling of the brain (cerebral edema). DKA occurs far more often in people with type I diabetes than in people with type II diabetes. But once you begin insulin therapy, you can almost always avoid it.

People tend to get DKA for two reasons. First, psychological or social pressures may cause people to stop taking their insulin. Teenagers may not be ready to take responsibilty for their own self-testing and injections. Emotionally or mentally disturbed adults also may drop their therapy.

Second, illness or stress can bring on DKA. When the body has to deal with a bacterial infection, a sickness such as the flu, or a stressful situation, hormones cause the liver to release stored glucose. These hormones also block the effects of insulin, so blood glucose can't enter the tissues. Fatty acids are used as an energy source instead. But the breakdown of fats yields chemicals called *ketones*, which can poison the blood with acidic products.

If you are sick enough that you can't eat, you may think, "I shouldn't take insulin today." Nothing could be more wrong. You need to maintain your normal routine; your body is producing extra glucose even though you aren't feeding it. You also need to test your urine ketones regularly on sick days. Higher than normal ketone levels are a sign of DKA and a warning bell to call the doctor. For more information on sick days, see Chapter 7, pages 140–144.

DKA is reversible in most cases. But the best way to fight it is to prevent it with careful blood glucose control.

Dealing With Hypoglycemia

An abnormally low blood glucose level is called hypoglycemia. (Compare this with hyperglycemia, an abnormally high blood glucose level.) For people with type I diabetes, hypoglycemia is a fact of life. On average, people with type I diabetes have one or two low blood glucose reactions every week.

Many things can cause too much of a drop in blood glucose levels. They include: too much insulin, too little food, a delayed meal, a poorly balanced meal (too little carbohydrate), illness, excess exercise, or alcohol on an empty stomach. Hypoglycemia usually occurs just before meals, after strenuous exercise, or when insulin is peaking; sometimes it occurs at night when you are sleeping.

The first response is to take a few raisins or pieces of hard candy or a glass of fruit juice. However, if your blood glucose level becomes so low that you lose consciousness, others must help you. You need a glucagon injection to bring you around. Otherwise, they need to find emergency help for you (see below). Your most important protection against hypoglycemia is testing your blood glucose levels. With this information, you can figure out how to balance food, activity, and insulin.

Low Blood Glucose Levels

You may have read that hypoglycemia occurs when your blood glucose levels fall below 50, 60, or 70 mg/dl. But you may know people with diabetes who have no symptoms of low blood glucose at 40 mg/dl and others who have symptoms in the normal blood glucose range. This is why it's hard to say that a low blood glucose reaction starts at a particular blood glucose level. In fact, you can develop symptoms of hypoglycemia when your blood glucose is falling rapidly but is still above 70 mg/dl. For example, if your blood glucose drops from 180 to 100 mg/dl rapidly, you might get chills or start sweating.

Hypoglycemic symptoms, although a clue, are not the full story. You must ask yourself, "Do I really have low blood glucose right now?" The answer is found by testing your blood glucose. If you don't test, you may tend to overtreat or overreact, causing soaring glucose levels and even weight gain. To start, ask your doctor what blood glucose levels to watch out for. You'll soon learn what level is too low for you.

You may have wondered why some people seem to have hypoglycemia more often than others. There are a couple of possible reasons. The liver of some people with diabetes does not release enough glucose to cover mild decreases in blood glucose levels. Thus, they don't have the built-in defense against hypoglycemia that others do. Another reason is that when you are on a multiple injection program or when you use an insulin pump, you often have a narrower range between your high and low blood glucose levels. Your highest blood glucose level may be 180 mg/dl and may only occur after you eat. If you exercise several hours after lunch, you may already be at 100 mg/dl, which may not be high enough to get you through your workout without a snack. You have a smaller margin of error when it comes to hypoglycemia. That's why it's so important to monitor your blood glucose a lot when you aim for tight glucose control.

If you try to maintain blood glucose levels that are a little high, to give you a cushion, you are more likely to avoid hypoglycemia. But you may be trading off the short-term risk of low blood glucose for the long-term risk of complications.

Symptoms

The symptoms associated with hypoglycemia are divided into two groups:

✦Autonomic symptoms: shakiness, nervousness, sweating, irritability, impatience, chills and clamminess, rapid heartbeat, anxiety, light-headedness, and hunger.

✦Neuroglycemic symptoms: sleepiness, anger, stubbornness, sadness, lack of coordination, blurred vision, nausea, tingling or numbness in the lips or tongue, nightmares, crying out during sleep, headaches, strange behavior, delirium, confusion, personality change, and unconsciousness.

The autonomic symptoms are called this because of the effect of low blood glucose on the autonomic nervous system of your body. These nerves control body functions without you thinking about them—for example, opening blood vessels, making your heart beat, and controlling breathing. The neuroglycemic symptoms are brought on by the reaction of the brain to prolonged low blood glucose.

Is It Really Hypoglycemia?

Each person's reaction to low blood glucose brings out a different set of these symptoms; you won't have them all. Generally, the autonomic symptoms are considered the early warning signs, but sometimes you may not notice them at all. They're easy to miss. You might already be anxious about a test or a new job. Your heart might be beating faster from excitement. Even some of the other symptoms are easier to blame on something else. Is your sadness due to a fight with a friend, or is it hypoglycemia? Don't wait to see if the symptoms go away. Only a blood glucose test can tell you for sure.

Certain health conditions make it even more difficult to sense a dip in blood glucose. If you have even mild autonomic neuropathy may not be able to detect early warning signs. Another reason you can miss the warning signals is if your glucose is under tight control. Then your symptoms might not be as dramatic because your glucose level is dropping slowly rather than rapidly. In addition, the longer you've had diabetes, the greater are your chances that you can miss early warning signs of low blood glucose. This loss of symptoms is called *hypoglycemia unawareness*. The cause is not yet known. However, it seems to be linked to longer length of time with diabetes rather than diabetic autonomic neuropathy. Even people without autonomic neuropathy can have it.

What if you are without your glucose testing equipment when you feel like your blood glucose is going low? Don't wait. When in doubt, always treat. A possible check, if you do not have your test strips, might be to take your pulse. Your heart beats faster with hypoglycemia. Of course, you will have to know what your normal resting heart rate is. If your heart rate is significantly high (for example, your resting heart rate is 76, but now it is over 100), you are likely to be having a reaction. If your heart rate does not come down after aerobic exercise, you might suspect hypoglycemia.

Certain symptoms can warn you that you have had hypoglycemia during the night. Do you find your pajamas and sheets damp in the morning? Have you had restless sleep and nightmares? When you wake up, do you have a headache or still feel tired? Are your morning fasting blood glucose levels high? Read about the Somogyi effect and the dawn phenomenon (below). You may have to check your blood glucose levels around 2 a.m. or 3 a.m. for a couple of days to pinpoint what is causing your glucose level to go up and down.

Testing your blood glucose level becomes even more important as your years with diabetes increase. If you have hypoglycemia unawareness and put yourself at risk for low blood glucose, you can have a severe hypoglycemic episode without warning. To avoid this, you'll want to choose a good program of glucose control, with regular self-monitoring of blood glucose levels.

Treatment

When you are having a low blood glucose reaction, your body needs glucose fast. You need to eat or drink a sugar that can be rapidly absorbed from your digestive tract into your bloodstream. By now, you probably have your favorite form of "pocket sugar" that you keep with you at all times. When you first notice a reaction, do a blood test if at all possible. Then take about 10 to 15 grams of glucose (about 1 fruit or 1 bread exchange). Retest your blood after 15 minutes. If the symptoms don't subside, you may need another helping of glucose.

Fast-acting sugars for mild hypoglycemia. You find similar foods on every list of fast sugar foods: half a can of regular soda, 4 ounces of orange juice, 5 to 7 LifeSavers, 6 jelly beans, 10 gumdrops, 2 large lumps or teaspoons of sugar, 2 teaspoons of honey or corn syrup, 2 tablespoons of raisins, a tube of Cake Mate decorator gel, 6 to 8 ounces of skim or 1% milk, 2 to 5 glucose tablets, depending on the brand. Each of these has about 10 to 15 grams of carbohydrate. For quick, certain relief, glucose tablets or gels (available at pharmacies) are best.

Everyone has a favorite way of treating hypoglycemia, but do you really know its exact effect on you? Try this: When your blood glucose is about 100 mg/dl or less, take your favorite fast-acting sugar. Wait 15 minutes. Then retest your blood. How much did your blood glucose rise—25, 30, 50, or more milligrams? You'll then know how to gauge your response to your level of hypoglycemia. You won't be as likely to overtreat and shoot your blood glucose up too high. And you won't be as likely to overeat and gain weight. Try this test with other choices. You may find that one food is faster and has more predictable results than another. Glucose tablets or gels probably are the most quickly absorbed of the group. And although milk takes longer to be absorbed, its effects last longer because it contains fat.

If your low blood glucose reaction has left you conscious but unable to chew and swallow, gels are a good choice. Someone may have to assist you by putting the gel inside your mouth between your cheek and gum.

If you are wondering whether to spend money on glucose tablets or gels, consider the following:

◆How fast it works. These products should work faster than food. Most of the food or drinks mentioned above contain sucrose, which your body must first turn into glucose. Glucose tablets and gels are already the simplest sugar, so the glucose should reach your blood more quickly.

✦Form. You probably won't be tempted to snack on these because the tablets or gels seem more like medications (although most don't taste that bad).

✦Cost. In most cases, the commercial glucose products cost more than foods containing fast-acting sugars.

These fast-acting sugars do not have a prolonged effect. You probably need to have a snack if you don't expect to have a normal meal for 30 minutes or so. You should not just keep eating these sugary foods because these foods may cause your blood glucose level to rebound to high levels. Avoid snack foods like candy bars, ice cream, cookies, and cake. The high fat and sugar content don't make them good choices. Good snack choices are foods with carbohydrate and protein, such as a half a sandwich. Or keep some graham crackers and low-fat milk or yogurt on hand.

Glucagon for severe hypoglycemia. If symptoms of hypoglycemia go unnoticed or unheeded, you could develop severe hypoglycemia. When your blood glucose level is very low for a long time, your brain does not get enough glucose, and you could become unconscious. This is a real emergency.

The best thing to do is avoid this situation to begin with. Be alert to your symptoms and treat yourself promptly. Also, your family, close friends, and coworkers need some training, from you or your health-care team, on the signs of severe hypoglycemia. If you are elderly, you are at an extra high risk for severe hypoglycemia.

Should you become unconscious, someone around you must take over. They should call for emergency help right away if they do not know how to inject glucagon. Your blood glucose level must be raised quickly. You may not be able to eat or drink anything; it could cause you to choke.

Glucagon is a hormone that raises the blood glucose level. It is injected just like insulin. Glucagon makes the liver release stored glucose, which revives someone who has become unconscious because of hypoglycemia. Glucagon does not work on someone with no glucose stores in the liver. This occurs in cases of starvation, or long surgery, or in people who are alcoholics.

Someone you trust needs to be trained in how to fill the special glucagon syringe and to inject you. Ask your family to go with you to a training session. Your doctor or nurse may show them how in a special office visit or they may suggest that all of you attend a class. Glucagon injection can cause vomiting, so your head needs to remain elevated above your stomach. You should respond to glucagon within 5 to 15 minutes. When you are awake enough to chew and swallow, take a substantial snack like half a sandwich. If there is no response to the first shot, whoever gave it should repeat the injection and get you to a hospital emergency room or call 911.

Special precautions may be necessary if you are pregnant and become unconscious. Because the fetus can be harmed more by high blood glucose and ketone levels and by drastic changes in blood glucose, your physician may suggest that only half of the normal dose of glucagon be given at first. Then wait 10 minutes to see if another shot is necessary. Because pregnant women are especially motivated to have tight control, they may be more likely to experience mild and moderate bouts of hypoglycemia. Frequent blood testing is the key to prevention.

You get glucagon by prescription only. Although you can mix your own glucagon and keep a filled syringe in the refrigerator for a month, it is easier to buy a glucagon emergency kit. The syringe in the kit is already filled with a diluting solution. Your pharmacist may have to order one for you. Make sure it has a long shelflife. Its effectiveness should not expire for about a year after you buy it.

Let your health-care team know whenever you have had to inject glucagon to reverse severe hypoglycemia. They also need to know if you have repeated bouts of mild hypoglycemia. Together you might find a pattern in your insulin, food, or activity routine that you have overlooked. Then you can make adjustments to help prevent these bouts of hypoglycemia.

You may want to consider investing in medical identification jewelry or carrying a medical identification card to give others information they would need to assist you when you are having difficulty with hypoglycemia. It would also be wise to have a snack on hand at all times, especially in your car and when you are exercising.

Special Precautions

Asking for help. Do you feel comfortable telling friends and a few colleagues at work, school, and even the gym about the possibility of your low blood glucose? During a hypoglycemic reaction, you can become so confused and irritable that you refuse help. Those around you may have to be persistent in the face of your denial. They can save you from a coma and a trip to the hospital by making sure you take some form of glucose quickly. Life is easier and safer if those with whom you spend the most time can spot a low blood glucose reaction and know what to do about it.

Teach your family and friends about treating hypoglycemia as they seem ready and able to learn. Remember how overwhelming the amount of information seemed to you at first. You don't have to teach them all by yourself. There are pamphlets and books, and perhaps your family would benefit from attending a class together.

You may feel embarrassed by symptoms that your hypoglycemia may cause. But being cranky and irritable at times is probably not too different from the way some of your friends act from time to time. And everyone can seem clumsy or confused once in awhile. Your friends and family will learn to be tolerant even when you are obnoxious and refuse help. You must be willing to let others know of the possibility of hypoglycemia and how to help.

Unnecessary chances. Although time alone is important for everyone, you need not take unnecessary chances. Why exercise late in the afternoon without taking a snack or checking your glucose levels? Why drive all day without stopping for lunch? Why swim alone? These are just a few examples of incidents where the possibility of hypoglycemia can be reduced. Be sensible. It's your life.

Exercise. You know exercise reduces your glucose levels. It doesn't make sense to work out really hard when you are totally alone. You could exercise or swim at a gym where others are around. Don't forget to have healthy snacks beforehand if you'll be burning a lot of calories. You'll find more on matching food needs to exercise in Chapter 9, pages 169–171.

If you develop hypoglycemia while exercising, STOP exercising. Don't say just one more lap or 5 more minutes. Do a blood glucose test and eat a fast-acting sugar if you need it. If you want to keep playing or working out, eat a snack and take a 15-minute break before starting back. Otherwise, your blood glucose level will drop quickly again. Studies have also shown that hypoglycemia is even more common 4 to 10 hours after exercise than near the time of the activity. Monitor your blood glucose levels to find out how your body reacts.

Sexual activity. If you are prone to hypoglycemia with exercise or during the night, you may experience a similar fall in blood glucose after sexual activity. If you are intimate at night, when your blood levels typically dip, you may need to adjust your insulin or have a snack before or after sexual activity.

Heart disease. If you have heart disease, discuss the link between hypoglycemia and heart disease with your doctor. Because hypoglycemia causes a rapid heart beat, your doctor may recommend that you maintain your blood glucose levels a little higher to reduce the chance of hypoglycemia.

Alcohol. If you drink alcohol, remember that it pushes down your blood glucose. Normally, if you start to have hypoglycemia, your liver will change stored starch to glucose, which helps protect you from too severe a reaction and gives you time to recognize and treat your low blood glucose. But alcohol interferes with this process. Read more about what to consider when you decide to drink alcohol in the Healthy Habits chapter.

Somogyi Effect and Dawn Phenomenon

Have you been surprised by high morning blood glucose readings after waking with hypoglycemic symptoms like sweating, restless sleep, nightmares, headaches, and exhaustion? You probably wondered how blood glucose could go up when you haven't eaten during the night.

Your body has a built-in defense mechanism to keep blood glucose from falling to deadly levels. When blood glucose is low, the hormones adrenaline, glucagon, growth hormone, and cortisol turn on the liver's mechanism to release stored carbohydrate (glycogen) as glucose in the blood. Your liver continues to respond to these hormones and keeps breaking down glycogen for about 3 hours. Your body tries to bounce back to normal levels. But for you—without insulin to control the glucose—the levels in the blood get too high, even without breakfast. You can also see an unhealthy ketone level in the urine as the body breaks down fat to make glucose.

Your body has another normal mechanism that wakes you up and gives you energy for your morning activities. This is called the *dawn phenomenon.* Your body responds to the wake-up call of the growth hormones and cortisol. These hormones depress the activity of insulin, allowing blood glucose to rise between about 2 a.m. and 8 a.m. Combined with the Somogyi effect, your blood glucose readings and ketone levels can be extremely high when you awaken.

What can you do to prevent this morning surge in blood glucose? You need to prevent the 3 a.m. dip. Here are some possible approaches: increase your bedtime snack or change your insulin routine so that it doesn't peak in the middle of the night. A better time for it to peak is when the wake-up hormones push up dawn blood glucose levels. People who use an insulin pump adjust their basal rate to anticipate these nightly ups and downs. Ask your doctor whether you should treat early-morning highs with extra before-breakfast insulin or less food at breakfast. Tell your doctor which choice you would prefer.

If you live alone, you may be justifiably afraid of having severe hypoglycemia when you are sleeping. Your best safeguard is to monitor your blood glucose levels before you go to sleep and occasionally during the night. If your blood glucose level is heading down, eat a small protein-filled snack.

Four

Intensive Diabetes Treatment

If you've been taking insulin for awhile, are you happy with your current way of doing things? Have you thought about monitoring your blood glucose levels more often? Have you thought about changing the type of insulin you use? Do you feel you should be using multiple injections or an insulin pump? If you've thought that improving your diabetes control would make your life better, maybe you're ready for tight glucose control.

Tight glucose control means keeping blood glucose levels as close to the nondiabetic range as possible. The blood glucose level of people without diabetes rarely goes over 140 mg/dl, even in the hours after a meal. The goal of intensive insulin therapy is to mimic the function of a normal pancreas by keeping your blood glucose as close to normal levels as possible. This means more than just changing your insulin strategy. Successful tight blood glucose control includes frequent blood glucose checks and more careful attention to food and exercise. In short, it's a big lifestyle change for most people with diabetes. However, the benefits are clear. The Diabetes Control and Complications Trial (DCCT), a 10-year study of people with type I diabetes, showed that tight glucose control reduces your chances of getting or of worsening diabetes-related problems of the eyes, nerves, blood vessels, and kidneys.

Day-to-day, intensive insulin therapy means testing blood glucose levels and using the results to make changes in insulin dose, diet, and exercise. Instead of your diabetes routine limiting your choices about when you eat, how much you eat, and when you can burn some calories, you gain flexibility by adjusting your insulin and food meal-to-meal to suit your choices.

You can't start intensive diabetes management on your own. You need support and information. First, you need an okay from your health-care team that, with your medical history, intensive insulin therapy will be a benefit to you. Ask your health-care team about their experience with and opinion of tight glucose control. It's possible that your doctor will feel more comfortable referring you to another doctor, perhaps a diabetes specialist with interest in tight control, or to a diabetes-care center that offers a complete management package. Second, you will need other teachers and supporters. Do you already have a dietitian and diabetes educator who can help you learn the skills you need for tight control? Your health-care team will need to be committed to teaching you how to interpret your blood glucose tests and adjust your insulin, food, and activity.

There are two basic types of intensive insulin therapy:

❖Multiple daily injections of Regular insulin, perhaps along with one or two injections of intermediate- or longer-acting insulin, and

❖Insulin pumps, which use phosphate-buffered Regular insulin.

Both of these approaches provide a baseline supply of longer-acting insulin to your body with short-acting Regular insulin before meals. With multiple injections of Regular insulin, you no longer need the intermediate insulin to cover meals. Thus, your meal-times and activities can be when you want them to be, not just when the insulin you injected says they should be. Graph 1 shows a typical pattern, but you can vary the timing of the Regular injections. This allows you to wait until an office meeting breaks up to eat lunch. With adjustments in your insulin dose and/or diet, you can jog today, play tennis tomorrow, and relax the next day with a good book. With careful attention to your blood glucose levels, you are not locked into a rigid schedule or diet anymore. This flexibility also comes in handy for people with unusual work schedules.

For example, instead of NPH mixed with your breakfast injection to cover lunch 4 to 6 hours later, you could take injections of Regular with both breakfast and lunch and schedule lunch when you want it.

Choosing between multiple injections or a pump is an individual decision. Both can provide good control of blood glucose levels and flexibility for your lifestyle. But you may feel more comfortable with one rather than the other. Your doctor may prefer to start

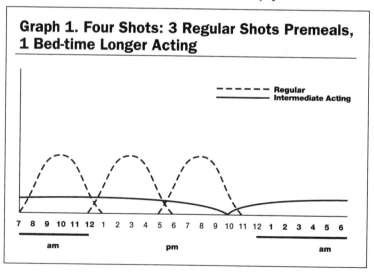

Graph 1. Four Shots: 3 Regular Shots Premeals, 1 Bed-time Longer Acting

- - - - - - Regular
———— Intermediate Acting

7 8 9 10 11 12 1 2 3 4 5 6 7 8 9 10 11 12 1 2 3 4 5 6

am   pm   am

whichever program you choose in the hospital so that your blood glucose can be monitored until it stabilizes.

If you inject insulin more often, you have chances to adapt the dose to your plans for the day. You not only have better control over your blood glucose but also over your lifestyle. Sound enticing? You say, "Yes, but ..." Well, intensive insulin therapy isn't for everyone. It requires someone motivated to do frequent blood tests and to learn how to adjust each insulin dose. It requires extra attention to prevent hypoglycemia. It also requires a greater awareness of how much and what you eat.

The insulin dose given before a meal (bolus) needs to match the amount of carbohydrate to be eaten at the meal. Plan on spending some time learning how to use your pump, how to change the insulin release rate, how to count carbohydrate in food, and how to deal with problems, like needle sites or catheters that won't stay in the skin. For more on insulin pumps, see Chapter 2, pages 34–38.

Multiple Daily Injections

Most multiple-injection programs for intensive insulin therapy call for three to five shots a day. There is a limit to how often anyone is willing to inject himself or herself in a day. You don't want to become so absorbed in blood testing and injecting that you can no longer do other things in life. So even if you could gain better control with six or eight shots, that is not reasonable for most people.

To start, your doctor will probably take your total daily insulin dose and divide it between the shots. Two standard multiple injection plans are:

♦Four shots of Regular insulin spaced throughout the day and night, before each meal and at bedtime.

✦One or two shots of intermediate- or long-acting insulin to establish a baseline level of insulin and a shot of Regular insulin before each meal.

If you follow the first plan, your doctor may, at first, recommend that you divide your Regular insulin dose equally among the four injections. Then, you will have to learn how to divide the doses to get the best coverage at mealtimes and through the night. If the bedtime dose is too large for you, you are likely to develop hypoglycemia about 2 a.m. to 3 a.m. as the insulin reaches its peak activity. If the bedtime dose is too small or is taken too early, you will not have enough insulin in your system to last until morning. If you have these problems continually, you will be better off including a longer-acting insulin in your plan.

With a long-acting insulin such as Ultralente added in the morning to a program of Regular shots before each meal, you have even greater flexibility. Because you have the safety net of the long-acting insulin, you can adjust your Regular insulin shots for the particular meal you eat. To start off on this program, your doctor may recommend that the Ultralente be two-fifths of your daily dose and each premeal injection be one-fifth. Because human Ultralente has a shorter action time than other long-acting insulins, you may need to split it into a morning and evening dose to ensure coverage around the clock.

Some multiple-injection programs are designed so that the intermediate- or long-acting insulin provides you with nighttime rather than daytime coverage. This is true when you take NPH or Lente insulin at bedtime. Then you will have to depend on evenly spaced (every 4 to 6 hours) Regular insulin for daytime coverage.

Insulin Pumps
....

If you choose to use a pump for tight glucose control, your doctor will need to divide your total daily insulin dose into two types of measures: a steady-release rate plus extra amounts of insulin for meals. The insulin dose given before a meal (bolus) needs to match the amount of carbohydrate to be eaten at the meal and the blood glucose level. Plan on spending some time learning how to use your pump, how to change the insulin-release rate, how to count carbohydrate in food, and how to deal with problems, like needle sites or catheters that won't stay in the skin. For more on insulin pumps, see Chapter 2, pages 34–38.

More About Blood Glucose Testing
....

You'll get the full advantages of this intensive approach by doing frequent blood glucose tests. The minimum number of tests is four: before each meal and at bedtime. Most people test after they eat as well, at least for the first couple of weeks, to get a feel for how well their premeal insulin dose is clearing away blood glucose. If you find your blood glucose level elevated before breakfast, you also need to test around 3 a.m.

Your results allow you to anticipate your body's needs and make adjustments in insulin. Perhaps you want to exercise. You'll know if you should reduce your Regular dose. Perhaps you want to go to a big Thanksgiving meal, but it's scheduled later than you normally eat. You have the long-acting insulin to carry you through until you take your Regular insulin before the feast.

It is not enough just to do the test. What's important is how you use the results. Together with your health-care team, you'll learn to calculate how much

Regular insulin you'll need before a meal to match its carbohydrate content. You'll learn how to spot patterns in your test results to make corrections. For example, you'll learn which insulin dose to adjust when you see before-breakfast readings that are high 3 days in a row.

It's a Process

Education

How will you learn everything you need to know about changing your insulin and food to meet your needs? You'll need more information about the nuts and bolts: for instance, how many units of insulin to take in response to particular test results. This trial and error process means quite a few phone calls to your doctor, nurse, and other health-care team members. And if you're like most, there will be times when frustrating events combine to make you want to quit. Again, calls to your health-care team can keep you going through tough times.

Hypoglycemia Awareness

Under tight glucose control, you will consistently have much lower blood glucose levels than you did before. That's why you need to relearn to balance your food intake and exercise under this new program. You may have been able to exercise before without being concerned about hypoglycemia because your glucose levels were higher than they are now. Naturally, you should not stop exercising but instead learn to take the appropriate precautions.

The DCCT set a target range of 70–120 mg/dl before meals and below 180 mg/dl after meals for participants on intensive insulin therapy. Compare your current readings to these targets. Are you already prone to hypoglycemia?

People who cannot recognize hypoglycemia, or who would be seriously harmed by low blood glucose reactions must be rigorous about testing their blood glucose levels frequently. People with heart problems, a history of stroke, or known inability to recognize the warning signs of hypoglycemia should be particularly cautious when using pumps. If you have diabetes-related problems with digestion (gastroparesis), which can cause unpredictable blood glucose swings, you may not be a good candidate for intensive insulin therapy. Ask your doctor's advice for your particular case.

A New View on Food

As you aim for tight blood glucose control, it will help to think about your meals in a new way. Rather than food servings or Exchanges, you may want to count the number of carbohydrates in a meal and target your insulin dose to match the carbohydrate load and your blood glucose level. Can your dietitian teach you how a meal will affect your blood glucose level and how to adjust your insulin dose? If not, find one who can.

People on intensive insulin therapy have a tendency to gain weight. Is that happening to you? To try to figure out why ask yourself some questions:

✦Do I eat too much in an attempt to prevent hypoglycemia?

✦Do I overtreat hypoglycemia when it occurs?

✦Do I take too much insulin and experience more hypoglycemia?

✦Do I eat more now than before?

It's easy for any of these things to happen to you if you don't watch out for them. Are you so carried away with the flexibility of intensive insulin therapy that you are skipping meals and then snacking all the time to make up for it? Remember that extra weight interferes with the body's ability to use insulin.

Actually, even if you don't eat more, you may gain a little weight because your body uses energy more efficiently once control is improved. It is not unusual to have a 5- to 10-pound weight gain after beginning an intensive regimen. One way to deal with weight gain is to reduce your calories. Snacks become less necessary for many people on intensive therapy. If you don't already exercise, begin a regular exercise program. If you do exercise already, try increasing your activity level. If your blood glucose levels begin to run low, talk to your health-care team about decreasing your insulin dose.

Five

Tools of the Trade

Diabetes management involves both art and science. The art consists of lifestyle skills—diet, exercise, and stress management. Science, in turn, supplies the medical basis for understanding the diabetes—and a high-tech toolbox. The diabetes toolbox consists of everything from the simple finger-stick device for blood drop samples to the latest blood glucose data management system. As with any set of tools, each must be chosen carefully to fit the user. You must also learn to use and maintain diabetes management tools. Your health-care team can help you with these challenges.

The best "catalog" for a diabetes toolbox is the American Diabetes Association *Buyer's Guide to Diabetes Supplies*, published every October in *Diabetes Forecast* magazine (see Resources, page 250). This guide lists and describes all available diabetes-care tools on the market. The next best references are the regular advertisements in the back of *Forecast*.

Blood Glucose Meters

In your war on high blood glucose levels, think of the blood glucose meter as your *diabetes intelligence service*. Only by knowing your enemy (abnormal blood glucose levels) can you decide which weapons to use (insulin, food, or exercise). After choosing the weapon, you can decide how to aim them (dosage or calories).

Blood glucose meters detect how much glucose is floating around in the blood by two basic methods. Some rely on a chemical—including one derived from the horseradish plant—that changes color when it comes in contact with glucose. Inside the meter, light is bounced off the developed color patch and "read." The color reading is computer-translated into a number (mg/dl) on the digital display.

Other meters exploit the fact that different amounts of glucose change blood's ability to conduct electrical currents. The patch contains an electrode that sets up an extremely weak current when in contact with a drop of blood. This current flows down the middle of the strip to be measured inside the meter.

Not all meters are created equal, however. The 1994 *Buyer's Guide to Diabetes Supplies* listed 18 models of blood glucose meter systems. All perform the basic job of reporting glucose levels in your blood. Some models, however, make more sense for you than others. To choose the right meter, consider such things as:

✦**Your dexterity**. Some devices are about the size of a credit card or even pen-sized. Others are more like a good-sized chocolate bar. If you have trouble with small hand and finger movements, choose a larger meter—although these may be slightly heavier to carry around, and you may want to avoid meters that require wiping blood from a strip. Finally, you will find it easier to use a brand of strip that comes in a vial, rather than individually wrapped in foil. The foil wrappings can be quite hard to remove.

✦**Your schedule**. Is your life a constant battle with the clock? Avoid devices that require wiping the blood drop and waiting up to 2 minutes. You can buy a meter that takes just 20 seconds of your time after the blood drop lands on the strip. These ultra-fast machines are especially useful in work and social situations, where it feels as if an extra 60 seconds really does make a difference.

✦**Your vision.** Two manufacturers (Boehringer Mannheim Corporation and AFB Product Center) offer products for visually disabled users. Both store 20 results, feature large-print displays and literature, and audio-cassette training materials. Touch-n-Talk II, a voice synthesizer, works with LifeScan's One Touch II meter. The "talking" device reads your results aloud to you and stores the data. Accu-Check II Freedom system gives various verbal cues and beeps to guide the user.

If you have some degree of color blindness, be sure that you have no trouble reading with the digital display.

If you have even some vision loss, you should make sure that a close companion or family member can help. Make sure they are trained in the use of your meter and the rest of the diabetes toolbox.

✦**Your hearing.** Some meters that require wiping of the blood sample emit a beep to signal when you should wipe. If you have a hearing loss, opt for the no-wipe models. With these you place the drop of blood on the strip and simply watch for the results.

✦**Support system.** If you are using a meter for the first time, consider one that offers a video that teaches you how to test. Make sure the company has a 24-hour 800 number to call when you have problems with the meter. Also check that your health-care professional is familiar with the model you purchase.

✦**User-friendliness.** Several features make meters easier to use. No-wipe models eliminate messy wiping of the blood sample and disposal. Those that need smaller-sized blood drops may be easier for those with poor circulation in their hands or who must test in cold environments.

◆**Accuracy and ease of care.** Each batch of testing strips is slightly different from the last. When you open a new batch, you must regulate—or calibrate—your meter to account for these differences. Then you will get accurate readings despite tiny differences in strips. Two machines calibrate completely by themselves. You don't have to do anything with a new batch of strips. On some models, however, procedures can be a little tedious. Some have a two-step procedure using a special strip. Instructions are usually included in every package of strips, so don't panic if you've lost your meter instruction manual.

Two procedures are necessary for ensuring accurate meter results. First, your meter should be calibrated with each new batch of test strips, as discussed above. Second, you must test your machine monthly for accuracy using a standard control solution. Like all machines, meters sometimes malfunction and give false results. This can have important health results. For instance, an elderly man with diabetes started having frequent urination, despite good meter results. His doctor brought up the possibility of prostate cancer, despite initial negative results. Fortunately, the worried man attended a diabetes-education program just after this disturbing news. The educators at the program discovered that his meter was showing normal blood glucose values when his real levels were high. He exchanged his meter for a new one and brought his blood glucose levels down. The urination problem turned out to be a sign of uncontrolled diabetes, not a prostate problem.

The moral of this story is to take your meter with

you for diabetes health-care visits. Take a meter reading within 5 or 10 minutes of having blood drawn for laboratory glucose tests. Compare the results. If your meter is off by more than 15 %, call the manufacturer for possible replacement. If you suspect your meter is not working correctly, you can also call the manufacturer's 800 number. You can order a vial of control solution to test the machine's accuracy. These solutions have a specific concentration of glucose for comparing to your meter's results.

✦**Meter size**. The pen- or card-sized meters slip easily into a shirt pocket when you're on-the-move. On the other hand, they get easily lost in a deep, dark handbag. The larger-sized meters stick out in both situations.

✦**Meter memory**. If you carry your meter around with you during the day, you may want one that stores more than one result in its memory. At night you can jot down the day's readings in your logbook. On the other hand, some meters store 20 or 30 results that you could copy into your record book and take to your diabetes health-care visit. A member of your health-care team can easily look over these results with you.

✦**Data-management systems**. Diabetes management is more than blood glucose readings. Meters that feature data-management systems can store many test results and information on time, date, insulin doses, and exercise. Two even serve as your alarm clock. The most advanced models can dump all this data into your health-care team's computer. Data-management system models are not that much more expensive than regular meters—$60–$100— often with big rebates. These systems can eliminate the log-book and provide you with a much more detailed picture of your diabetes management. Before you buy a system, check to see if your health-care team uses one too; make sure your system is compatible with theirs. Also, call the manufacturer's 800 number and ask someone in customer service exactly what you're getting.

✦**Language.** Some meter systems can display in English, Spanish, or up to seven other languages.

✦**Battery and machine replacement.** Just like flashlights and TV remote controls, meters need batteries. Each model handles batteries differently. For some, you buy the replacement battery and insert it yourself. These can be fairly expensive and hard to find; others are standard electronic equipment batteries. Check out ahead of time where you can obtain a battery or have one on hand before you need it. At least one company replaces batteries, and some simply replace the whole meter. With the latter you call the 800 number and the manufacturer sends you a new meter by express delivery. They supply an envelope to ship back the old one. You miss testing for no more than 2 days. You can use visually read blood glucose strips during that time (see below).

✦**Blood contamination.** If you have a blood-borne illness such as HIV, you will want to avoid accidental contamination with splashing or disposal of wipe materials. Consider late-model meters with no-wipe strips that actually absorb the whole blood drop.

✦**Convenience.** If you commute, buy two meters (that use the same brand of strip). Keep one at home and the other in your desk drawer at work. This saves the nuisance of moving one back and forth. Even more important, you avoid the hazard of forgetting the meter at one end or the other.

✦**Your insurance coverage.** Your diabetes center, insurance program, or company health plan may specify certain meters. Check this out before you purchase a meter. Also find out if you are covered for the strips.

✦**Your budget**. Be sure to check the cost of strips before you buy a meter. In the long run, the strips will cost you more money than the meter itself. You may want to buy a meter that can be used with compatible generic-brand strips that cost about 30% less, but be aware that these strips may not be as accurate as the strips made specifically for your meter.

Don't buy a high-end blood glucose data-management system unless you can afford the extra $30–$50. Most people can get along with a good logbook.

If you are a computer buff, you can also buy computer programs that take meter data-management systems one step further. You enter the data (by hand, or electronic download from your meter) and the program can provide trend analysis, averages, graphs, printouts, and more. Check ads in *Diabetes Forecast* or the Shopper's Guide for these products.

Test Strips

Independent manufacturers now produce generic, color-development test strips that can be used with brand-name meters. They are still working on the electronic strips. You can save up to 30 % of the cost of brand-name strips this way. The *Diabetes Forecast* Shopper's Guide and ads list these strips.

Visually Read Glucose Strips

Circumstances sometimes prevent you from using blood glucose meters. This would be rare in the United States, but is not unusual in developing countries where modern supplies are in short supply. In such circumstances you might have to fall back on visually read blood or urine strips. Visually read strips also come in handy if your meter malfunctions for some reason. These are read by comparing color developed on the strip to a color chart printed on the strip vial.

The color patches for visually read strips progress in increments of 20–30 mg/dl. Readings can be "educated guesswork." Some people, with years of experience, can read visually read strips almost as accurately as a meter. Visually read strips cost about the same as color-developed meter strips.

There are also visually read urine strips to tell you how much glucose is in your urine. Unfortunately, testing urine glucose is a poor way to tell your blood glucose level. First, you don't get measurable amounts of glucose in your urine until blood levels are high. Second, urine glucose levels tell you how much glucose was in your blood 2 or 3 hours ago. This information is not useful for deciding insulin dosages, or even evaluating your overall treatment program.

When you have nothing else available, use urine strips to test your urine glucose. But keep in mind that the readings may not reflect your current blood glucose level. Also remember that urine glucose readings can be altered by vitamin C, aspirin, fluid intake, moisture, and failure to completely empty your bladder.

If you are color-blind, check with your health-care team to see what brand of strip will work best for you.

Visually Read Strips for Urine Ketones

There is an important visually read strip test that offers the only way of knowing if your body is burning body fat instead of glucose. Often your first tip comes when a family member reports that a fruity smell is on your breath (ketones in the air). When everyone in the family has a stuffy nose, though, you'd better have ketone strips (or test tablets) on hand.

Ketones can show up from too much food (high blood glucose), too little food (low blood glucose), and insulin reactions. If you have high ketones in the morning, you might have slept through an insulin reaction.

Always test for ketones when
+your blood glucose readings are over 240 mg/dl
+you are ill (high fever, bouts of vomiting, or diarrhea)
+during pregnancy, daily before breakfast (fasting)
+during acute stress (physical or psychological).

Other times to do a ketone check are when you see an upward-moving trend in your glucose levels, have chronic tiredness, fruity breath, vomiting, breathing difficulties, or if you're having a hard time paying attention.

Ketone results aren't given in precise units, such as "dl" or "mg." Like eggs at the grocery store, the side of the vial reads from "0" and "trace" to "small, moderate, and large." Some just score with "+" signs. If you read anything more than "0" with an occasional "trace," ask your health-care team what levels are dangerous for you. You may need to take action.

If you have high ketones along with high blood glucose levels, you'll want to lower them by
+taking additional insulin, using 1 unit for every 25 mg/dl your blood glucose levels are over 250 mg/dl.
+Drinking plenty of water to flush out the ketones.
+Avoiding exercise. Exercise just causes more fat-burning due to insufficient insulin.

Ask your health-care team *in advance* what you should do (especially regarding insulin). This way you can take action on your own.

If you are color-blind, check with your health-care team to see what brand of strip will work best for you.

Finger-Sticking Devices and Lancets

Many blood glucose meter kits come with a finger-sticking device and a few lancets. (A few have the lancet built in to the meter.) If this device works for you, fine. Be aware that there are several kinds of devices and lancets. The devices often have two caps that control how deep the lancets poke into your finger. Use the shallowest poke possible to draw blood—it hurts less, and cuts down on scarring of your fingers. Devices without adjustment may poke/hurt too much for you. Shop around for another.

Some people use lancets without the automatic lancing device to sample their blood. This takes some practice. If you can do it, you'll save a little money and not have to tote a lancet around.

If you have dexterity limitations, look for an automatic lancing device that resets easily with a simple push-pull movement.

Record-Keeping

The logbook? This low-tech equipment is often overlooked as an important piece of the diabetes toolbox. Everybody gets one free with their first meter. After that, they can be surprisingly hard to find. Many pharmacies and chains don't carry them "because the meter manufacturers provide them." Mail-order houses carry logbooks however. If you have trouble finding them, grab a few when you do see the rare specimens on the shelf. Also, call the 800# for your meter company and request more.

People who face complications with diabetes and other conditions might consider buying a spiral-bound notebook instead. The advantage of these is that you can list a variety of symptoms or situations relevant to your medical condition. Notebooks also offer lots of room to write for people whose fingers might be a little stiff.

Odds 'n Ends

Everyone with diabetes should round out their tool kit with a few other items. One is the carrying case for diabetes supplies. Have you ever tried to stuff your meter, syringes, insulin, alcohol wipes, and so forth into a purse or briefcase? If you have, you'll know why you need a special carrying bag. These cases do two things for you. First, they organize all your supplies. Second, they insulate your insulin from hot or cold temperatures. They also separate your diabetes supplies from other baggage (avoiding the diabetic beginner's nightmare of having supplies lost in a suitcase gone astray at the airport).

In your carrying case—and your purse, your car, your bathroom, and your nightstand—be sure you have glucose tablets or some other form of fast acting sugar. Glucose tablets or gels come in handy when your blood glucose level plummets and you find it difficult to get to the refrigerator for orange juice. The tablets are easy to handle, and they work within minutes. You're less likely to overconsume glucose tablets than if you decide to use chocolate ice cream instead. You should experiment to see which of the fruit-flavored tablets taste best to you.

Finally, your tool kit should include personal identification that identifies you and your medical condition in case you become unconscious or injured. The most famous medical ID comes from the nonprofit Medic Alert Foundation, which keeps updated medical information available on computer

24 hours a day (see Resources, page 262). Other information cards, pendants, bracelets, and tags have the information printed right on them. Gold/silver designer ID is now available, as are kid-sized/kid-colored products. These can be in your tool kit when you're not wearing them.

Shopping Around

Shopping for your diabetes tools takes some practice. If you are in the market for a new meter, for instance, check your insurance or Medicare coverage. Currently, insulin-dependent Medicare beneficiaries are covered for monthly glucose-testing supplies and one meter per year. Your insurance may cover the meter, the strips, or just one.

Meters are usually deeply discounted by the manufacturer. To get the latest information on the model you're interested in, call the manufacturer's 800 number and talk to someone in customer service.

If your insurance offers meters and strips through a mail-order program, you needn't worry about bargain-hunting. However, you will need to get a physician's prescription to be reimbursed for the meter and strips.

If you're on your own financially, check *Diabetes Forecast* Shopper's Guide. You'll probably find a bargain, especially in shopping for strips (remember the generics). Most ads and mail-order houses offer better prices than you'll find at the local pharmacy. The pharmacy also offers a much smaller selection of equipment. If you have a good relationship with your pharmacist, however, you may ask him or her to order the machine you want.

A critical aspect of mail-order houses is timing. Be sure to order your strips, insulin, and other equipment at least 2 weeks in advance. Waiting until the last moment will leave you high and dry for medication and test supplies. Also, if you are insured, starting up with a mail-order house takes additional time up front. They must confirm your insurance coverage before filling your first order.

Diabetes supply specialty stores offer another shopping option. To find one, call your local ADA chapter, or check in the phone book under "Medical Supplies" or "Diabetes." If you're lucky enough to have one in the neighborhood, you may be able to one-stop-shop for many nonprescription items. Some pharmacies specialize in diabetes supplies, carrying a large number of brands of meters and other supplies. In addition to medical supplies, you may find low-calorie foods, candies, books, and information on local diabetes events and organizations. In diabetes shops, you can actually compare models, ask questions, and receive training on complicated tools.

Grocery store and chain pharmacies carry diabetes supplies. If the store in your neighborhood doesn't have your brand of strips or meters, ask the pharmacist if a sister store does. Stores in neighborhoods with more elderly people, for instance, may carry more brands of supplies.

Stretching Diabetes Dollars

Living with diabetes takes money, sad to say. Your monthly investment in equipment and supplies can eat a major hole in your budget. Here are a few tips to save money:

✦ Test blood glucose on a regular schedule. Skipping tests may be a false economy...you could end up spending much more if your diabetes gets out of control.

✦ Consider using syringes more than once. There is no evidence that reusing syringes increases your chances for infection, if you do it right. Ask your health-care team if it's safe for you and how to care for your syringes.

✦Use generic strips if you have the right meter.

✦Go for those rebate and trade-in discounts on meters.

✦Keep equipment clean and dry.

Six

Diabetes Complicatons

Most of us spend little time thinking about the future. We focus on the here and now. What's for dinner? How late will we have to work today? How long can we put off doing our laundry? If you have type I diabetes, you have even more concerns about the present: cooking meals on your plan, exercising, testing your blood glucose, and taking insulin.

Diabetes is complicated enough—without the thought of complications in the future. Complications are health problems related to diabetes, such as kidney disease, blindness, or nerve damage. Maybe you shrug your shoulders and say there's no point in looking ahead to health problems. After all, complications don't strike everyone with type I diabetes, and it's not easy to think about such large troubles.

But there's good reason to think ahead. If you make changes in your life now, you'll lower your chances of getting complications down the road. This advice is backed up by an important recent study. The Diabetes Control and Complications Trial (DCCT) spent 10 years looking at more than 1,400 people with type I diabetes. Those people who worked to keep their blood glucose levels as close to normal (nondiabetic) as possible ended up with less eye disease, less kidney disease, and less nerve damage. They had to test and inject insulin more often each day, but their extra work paid off. They cut their risk of these complications by more than half. You can read more about tight control in Chapter 4. It's also a good idea to discuss this option with your doctor.

The Glucose Connection

You may decide to try tight control, or you may decide it's not right for you. Either way, any steps you take to keep your blood glucose levels more normal will help you avoid damage to your eyes, kidneys, and nerves.

Having too much glucose in your blood affects most of the parts of your body. The extra glucose sticks to proteins in your blood. It stops the cells that keep your blood vessels healthy from doing their job. Small blood vessels that carry blood throughout the body can get narrower or blocked so they are damaged and blood flow is limited. It can also damage nerve cells and delay, change, or halt electrical messages. Your body tries to rid itself of the excess glucose by adding it to your urine, cycling more and more blood through your kidneys.

Even though you take insulin, your blood glucose levels are still higher than normal *some* of the time. Adopting a plan of tight control, or at least working harder to control your diabetes, means that you spend less time with high blood glucose. You are closely matching your insulin dose to your blood glucose levels. Rather than floating around in your blood damaging things, glucose goes straight into your cells where it can do its duty: producing the energy you need.

Other Healthy Habits

So you're working on blood glucose control. Can you

do anything more to ward off complications?

Yes, plenty. In fact, you may be taking steps to prevent or reduce complications without even knowing it. That's because many of the steps are good advice for people without diabetes, too. Everywhere you turn, you hear "watch your blood pressure," "eat less fat," "stop smoking," and "exercise!" Don't deafen your ears to these warnings. They are even more important for people with diabetes than they are for the general public. Because your risk of health problems is already higher, you need to take every chance to lower it.

Don't smoke. You probably already know that smoking can cause a wide and frightening range of lung disorders. But smoking has another, diabetes-related effect. It damages your heart and circulatory system by narrowing your blood vessels over time. When blood flow to cells is limited, they can die. This damage can lead to heart disease, impotence, and amputation. If you smoke now, talk to your health-care team about methods to help you quit.

Eat healthy foods. Your doctor or dietitian has probably suggested a meal plan with little fat and cholesterol, lots of complex carbohydrates, and a moderate amount of protein. If you have high blood pressure, you may also have been told to cut down on salt. Eating wisely has benefits far beyond keeping your blood glucose under control. It reduces your risk of cardiovascular and kidney disease.

Keep your blood pressure down. High blood pressure (hypertension) puts a strain on your body, especially your blood vessels and kidneys. You can help lower your blood pressure by losing weight, exercising, and limiting the amount of alcohol you drink. Your doctor may also prescribe medication to help bring your blood pressure down.

Exercise. People with type I diabetes reap three benefits from exercise. First, exercise helps delay or stop disease of the heart and large blood vessels. Second, exercise helps clear glucose out of your blood so that cells can use it for energy. This lowers blood glucose levels and can lower the total amount of insulin you need. Third, exercise gives a boost to your efforts to control your blood glucose. The same motivation that helps you exercise regularly will help you with your daily self-monitoring of blood glucose.

Handling Complications

All your hard work can't guarantee you will be free of complications. Factors you don't control—such as your age, your race, and your genes—influence your risk.

If you get a complication, you may have many of the same feelings you had when you were first diagnosed with type I diabetes—anger, fear, guilt, or denial. You may have thought that you had good diabetes control all figured out, and it may be frustrating to find you now have to make another effort. You may feel overwhelmed that on top of the ordinary stresses of life and having diabetes, you have new health problems to contend with.

Treatments for diabetes complications are constantly becoming more effective. It's probably a bad idea to get your information about complications from friends or relatives. They may remember therapies from years ago, not modern ones.

The rest of this chapter explains some of the most common complications of diabetes, centering on ways to prevent them and treat them.

✦Cardiovascular Disease

✦Retinopathy (eye disease)

✦Nephropathy (kidney disease)

✦Neuropathy (nerve disease)
✦Infections
✦Diabetes and Sex
✦Amputations
✦Impotence
✦Other Complications

Cardiovascular Disease

Cardiovascular disease can go by many names—arteriosclerosis, "hardening of the arteries," peripheral vascular disease, coronary artery disease, and stroke—but they all describe problems with the heart and circulatory system. The flow of blood through the body provides all the oxygen, glucose, and other substances needed to run your body and keep its cells alive.

Narrowing or clogging of blood vessels limits blood flow and can kill tissues. People with diabetes are more likely to get a condition which stiffens, narrows, or clogs blood vessels, called *arteriosclerosis*.

Diabetes also seems to change blood chemistry, making heart disease more likely. Diabetes changes the number and makeup of proteins that deliver lipids to cells. These lipoproteins will usually return to normal if you achieve good control. Diabetes also affects blood cells known as platelets. They may churn out too much of a chemical that constricts blood vessels and causes clotting. And, to add insult to injury, once an artery is damaged, poor blood flow due to uncontrolled diabetes can slow its healing.

Cardiovascular disease can cut off blood supply to the heart and brain. If blood to the heart is slowed for a time, the pain that results is called angina. A complete, long-lasting stoppage of blood is a heart attack. When blood to the brain is stopped, a stroke results. When blood in the arteries in the legs is blocked, the leg pain that goes along with walking is called *intermittent claudication.*

Prevention

Five actions—controlling blood glucose, stopping smoking, eating low-fat foods, avoiding high blood pressure, and exercising—will bring down your risk of cardiovascular disease dramatically. They will help your large blood vessels remain wide open for the flow of blood.

Treatment

If you get cardiovascular disease, the five steps for prevention can still help you. They may slow or stop the progression of the disease. A diet low in cholesterol and saturated fat is especially good. Eating more fiber may be another way to lower your levels of cholesterol and lipids called *triglycerides.*

When these measures fail, surgery is possible to open blocked blood vessels. One kind of minor surgery, called *balloon angioplasty*, uses a balloon at the tip of a tube to open the vessels. The surgeon inflates the balloon where the artery is blocked to open up the vessel. Another minor surgery, called *arthrectomy*, opens the blockage by boring a hole through it. Laser surgery melts away blockages with an intense beam of light. These surgeries require little recovery time.

A more severe blockage calls for more serious surgery. *Arterial bypass surgery* creates a detour for blood to flow around the blockage. Surgeons remove part of a large artery from the chest wall or a vein from the leg and sew it above and below the blocked segment. Blood flows through the new vessel instead of the blocked one.

There are treatments for most other types of cardiovascular disease too. Intermittent claudication may be relieved by exercise, drug therapy, and/or surgery. Strokes usually call for a combination approach: normalizing blood glucose, blood pressure, and blood lipid levels; helping the person recover mental and physical abilities; and giving drugs to control blood clotting. Sometimes, surgery is needed. Treatment of angina aims at reducing the amount of oxygen the heart tissue requires and increasing the oxygen going to the heart. People with diabetes and angina are advised to get more exercise, normalize their blood glucose levels, and lose weight. They also may take drugs or need surgery.

Retinopathy

Retinopathy is a disease of the tiny blood vessels that supply the retinas, the "movie screens" at the back of your eyes where the images you see are projected. When it begins, you don't notice diabetic retinopathy. It takes an exam by an eye doctor to see the changes in the blood vessels. Detected early, retinopathy can be slowed or stopped altogether.

In one form of diabetic retinopathy, blood vessels may close off or weaken and leak blood, fluid, and fat into the eye. This form is called *nonproliferative (background) retinopathy*. It may lead to blurry vision, but it does not cause blindness unless there is leakage in the macula.

Nonproliferative retinopathy can progress to a more serious, rarer condition called *proliferative retinopathy*. When this happens, new blood vessels sprout in the retina. That may sound good, but the new vessels grow out of control. They are fragile, so they rupture easily with high blood pressure, exercise, or even while sleeping. Blood may leak into the fluid-filled portion of the eye in front of the retina, impairing sight. Scar tissue may form on the retina as well. When the scar tissue shrinks, it can pull the retinal layers apart. This damages sight; images look as though they are projected on a sheet flapping in the breeze. Glaucoma may go along with proliferative retinopathy. This increased pressure in the eye can be treated if it is spotted early on.

Retinopathy can also affect the macula of the eye, the central portion of the retina that gives us sharp vision for seeing fine detail. The swelling of the macula, called *macular edema*, can limit vision and lead to blindness.

Prevention

There are two well-proven ways to lower your risk of blindness from eye disease. First, get a yearly eye exam through dilated pupils from an eye doctor once you reach age 30 (or if you're under age 30 but have had diabetes for 5 years). Finding problems in their early stages allows for much better treatment and greatly reduces the chances of blindness.

Second, get your blood glucose levels as near to normal as possible. The Diabetes Control and Complications Trial (DCCT) was most conclusive about the benefits of tight control when it came to retinopathy. People practicing tight control significantly reduced their chances of getting retinopathy or having their retinopathy worsen.

Treatment

Oddly enough, the best treatment for people with diabetes in danger of losing their sight involves a laser—an intense beam of light. An ophthalmologist aims the laser at the retina to create hundreds of tiny burns in it. The burns destroy abnormal blood vessels, patch leaky ones, and slow the formation of new fragile vessels. This procedure is called *photocoagulation*. In people with high-risk proliferative retinopathy or macular edema, photocoagulation can usually prevent blindness.

Photocoagulation may not work if the retina has bled a lot or has detached. In these cases, surgery called *vitrectomy* can remove the blood and scar tissue, stop bleeding, replace some of the vitreous (the clear, jelly-like fluid in the eye) with salt solution, and repair the detached retina.

If you need either of these procedures, choose an ophthalmologist who specializes in retinal disease and has patients with diabetes. And as always, the earlier the procedure is done, the better.

If laser treatment or vitrectomy fail to restore vision, low-vision aids can often help people regain the ability to read the paper, do paperwork, or watch TV.

Nephropathy

Your kidneys work 24 hours a day to cleanse your blood of toxic substances made by or taken into the body. These toxins enter the kidney by crossing the walls of small blood vessels that border it. In people with nephropathy, these blood vessels, called capillaries, cease to be good filters. They become blocked and leakier at the same time. As a result, some wastes that should be removed stay in the blood, and some protein that should stay in the blood is removed.

No one knows exactly why diabetes and nephropathy go together so often, but they do. Some people with newly diagnosed type I diabetes may have an excess of protein in their urine temporarily. But more obvious symptoms of kidney disease take a long time to appear. The kidneys have so much extra filtering ability that 80% of the kidney must be damaged before noticeable problems appear.

Prevention
Once the kidneys are damaged, they cannot be

healed. So you must take care to prevent nephropathy or to slow the progress if you have it. Keep your blood glucose under control; the DCCT showed that keeping blood glucose near normal helped people avoid nephropathy. Treat high blood pressure, which can damage the delicate capillaries in your kidneys. Two ways to help avoid high blood pressure are to keep a healthy body weight and to eat less salt. If kidney damage is advanced, doctors will prescribe drugs and a low protein diet to lower blood pressure.

Treatment

Very advanced kidney disease means that filtration is greatly disrupted and the kidneys are failing. This condition is *end stage renal disease*. At this point, there are only two treatment options: dialysis and kidney transplantation.

Dialysis uses a substitute for a kidney to clean the blood. One type of dialysis, called *hemodialysis*, removes the blood from an artery (usually in the arm), filters it through a machine, and returns it to a vein. Treatments most often take place at a treatment center, three times a week for 2 1/2 to 4 hours. Trained caregivers may also perform hemodialysis at home. Hemodialysis can lower your red blood cell count, so be aware that you may have to adjust your blood glucose meter to give accurate glucose readings. But by all means, keep testing your blood glucose level.

The other type of dialysis uses the abdominal cavity as the filtering site. In *peritoneal dialysis*, a tube called a catheter is surgically placed in the abdomen, and a solution is poured into it to collect waste products from the blood. The exchange occurs across the peritoneum, or abdominal sac. After a few hours, the solution containing wastes from the blood is drained out of the abdomen. This method can be done manually by the person or by a machine overnight. Its main drawback is the risk of infection in the abdominal cavity.

Dialysis is generally not as effective as kidney transplantation. Transplantation offers the best chance for an active life because the new kidney functions as well as the your two old ones did before disease. A relative may be willing to donate a healthy kidney or a kidney may become available from someone who has just died. People often go on dialysis while waiting for a transplant.

Transplantation does have its drawbacks, however. It is major, expensive surgery. It requires you to take drugs that prevent the immune system from rejecting the new kidney. What's more, the new kidney will face the same pressures that the old ones did. Without good prevention and good blood glucose control to keep the kidney healthy—and sometimes even with prevention—the new kidney may fail too.

Neuropathy

Too much blood glucose damages the nervous system. The brain and spinal cord are not affected, but damaged nerves either can't send messages, send them at the wrong time, or send them too slowly. If you have damaged nerves, or diabetic neuropathy, you may feel pain in your hands or feet. If nerves to your internal organs are involved, you may have trouble digesting food or occasionally lose control over your bladder or bowel. Often symptoms of diabetic neuropathy come and go, and are severe for a short period of time. Good blood glucose control can help you avoid or improve these symptoms.

Researchers still aren't sure why high blood glucose harms nerves. It's possible that glucose-coated proteins damage nerves, or high levels of glucose may upset the chemical balance inside nerves. The damage can be indirect, if the blood supply to the nerves is limited and nerves don't receive enough oxygen. Single nerves may also get squeezed by the tissues surrounding them. In this way, injury to a part of the body can lead to neuropathy.

Prevention

Good blood glucose control seems to protect you from nerve disease. Keeping the blood vessels supplying nerves healthier will also protect you; in addition to good blood glucose control, it's a good idea to exercise, stop smoking, and eat right. Studies have also shown that a healthy diet, rich in food sources of vitamins and minerals, keeps the nervous system in good working order. Alcohol is directly toxic to nerves, so limiting alcohol intake is a good idea.

Types and Treatment

Distal symmetric polyneuropathy. Neuropathy can strike nerves in most parts of the body. It may affect the arms, hands, legs, or feet on both sides of the body. This condition is called *distal symmetric polyneuropathy*. It may make you feel numb and lose sense of temperature and the position of your limbs. On the other hand, you could feel shooting or stabbing pains, burning, tingling or prickling, or weakness. You should always wear shoes and check your feet and shoes every day because a loss of feeling means you might step on something and injure your foot without knowing it and get an infection.

Treatment. The pain of distal symmetric polyneuropathy will often vanish after a few months or a year of good blood glucose control. Your doctor can help you treat it by suggesting exercises and prescribing oral medications and surface creams to rub into areas that are painful. One new cream, capsaicin, is made from an extract of hot peppers. It often works for people who do not respond to more traditional treatments. Its stinging may merely distract you from the pain of neuropathy. But some researchers think it directly interrupts pain signals from the damaged nerves.

Antidepressants such as imipramine can also relieve nerve pain. In addition, they may help people with the depression, anxiety, and insomnia that sometimes accompany neuropathy. Mexiletine, a heart drug and antiepileptic drug, also seems to ease nerve pain. Clonazepam may help relieve symtoms. Stretching may relieve pain in the muscles. Narcotic painkillers are usually not helpful.

Much new research in neuropathy focuses on a group of drugs called *aldose reductase inhibitors* (ARIs). These drugs stop fructose, a sugar, and sorbitol, a sugar alcohol, from building up and thus, damaging nerves. If studies prove that ARIs are an effective treatment for the pain of neuropathy, they may join the list of prescription medications used to treat it.

Focal neuropathy. A rarer condition, *focal neuropathy* centers on a single nerve or group of nerves. It may arise when blood supply to a nerve shuts off because a vessel becomes blocked. It may also happen when a nerve becomes squeezed. It can injure nerves that sense touch and pain as well as nerves responsible for moving muscles. Fortunately, it usually goes away fairly fast, within 2 weeks to 18 months, after better blood glucose control is achieved.

Carpal tunnel syndrome is one focal neuropathy

seen more often in people with diabetes. The median nerve of the forearm can be squeezed in its passageway, or tunnel, by the carpal bones at the wrist. The syndrome is three times more common in women than in men. It may cause tingling, burning, and numbnes so that you may drop objects without realizing you have. Fortunately, carpal tunnel syndrome is not permanent. You can treat it with good blood glucose control, medications, or surgery to remove tissues squeezing the nerve.

Autonomic neuropathy. Neuropathy can damage nerves that you don't control voluntarily, such as those to your internal organs. This condition is called *autonomic neuropathy*. It may slow down stomach and gut muscles, leading to constipation, a feeling of fullness, and even diarrhea, nausea, or occasional vomiting. Damaged nerves to the bladder may cause muscle weakness so that it cannot get completely empty. Then the bladder will occasionally empty involuntarily. Because urine remains in the bladder for a long time, it can cause urinary tract infections. And it can give misleading results when you test the urine for glucose. Men may slowly lose the ability to have an erection, even though they still have sexual desire. Women, too, may have decreased sexual response because of vaginal dryness. Blood pressure may fall when you stand, making you feel dizzy or lightheaded. Nerves to the skin may cause too much or too little sweating or very dry skin.

Nerves to the heart may fail to speed up or slow down your heart rate in response to exercise. This is one reason to get a check-up before you begin any program of exercise. If you can't trust your heart rate to reflect your exertion, you will not be able to use standard ways to find target heart rate during and after a workout.

Treatment. There are different treatments for the different effects of autonomic neuropathy. Digestion problems take patience and some trial and error to treat. You may avoid them by changing your eating habits. Eat small, frequent meals instead of large ones, and choose higher-fiber and lower-fat foods. Some medications can increase emptying of gut and eliminate the feeling of fullness, constipation, and diarrhea.

Incontinence, or urine leakage, can be treated with training in bladder control and timed urination by a planned bladder-emptying program. Urinate by the clock every two hours rather than waiting for the feeling of fullness. Men may have to learn to urinate sitting down. Applying pressure over the bladder may be helpful. If these steps don't work, taking oral medications, learning to use a catheter, and having surgery can work. Fecal incontinence (passing stool involuntarily) is treated the same way, with medicine for diarrhea and biofeedback training.

Sudden drops in blood pressure on standing can be treated as well. You may need to stop drinking alcohol and stop taking certain medications, such as diuretics. Your health-care team may advise you to take medications for low blood pressure, raise the salt content of your diet, change your sleeping position, and improve your general health. Your blood volume goes up with medication, retains more salt and water, and may result in swollen ankles or fingers for you. Be careful when you stand up, and try not to stand still for long periods of time to prevent fainting. When you get up in the morning, sit on the edge of the bed and dangle your feet for 5 minutes before you stand up.

You can read about specific treatments for sexual problems related to neuropathy at the end of this chapter.

Neuropathy can often start a cascade of complications. One effect often seen in people with long-standing diabetes is known as Charcot's joint. Most often, this disorder strikes weight-bearing joints, such as the ankles. It all starts with a loss of feeling and thinning of the bones in the feet. This leads to a painless fracture. The injury doesn't cause pain, so it doesn't get treated properly and the person keeps walking on it. Muscle shrinking (atrophy) and joint damage follow. Without treatment, the damage becomes severe enough to deform the foot. Walking is then impossible. Early treatment is key to healing Charcot's joint. It involves keeping weight off the joint and wearing special footwear. If you have unexpected swelling of a foot, let your doctor see it.

More than 50 conditions other than diabetes may cause or promote neuropathy. Drinking alcohol, for instance, makes neuropathy worse. Your primary-care doctor needs to find out whether or not the neuropathy is linked to diabetes. He or she may test nerves or muscles to sort out the cause.

Infections

Diabetes makes fighting infections difficult. Killing invading bacteria and fungi is the job of the immune system. But diabetes can weaken infection-fighting cells, and blood flow may be so slowed that these cells have difficulty reaching the infection site. Meanwhile, some of the invaders thrive on the extra glucose in the blood, and with high blood glucose, white blood cells cannot work properly. People with diabetes tend to have more infections everywhere: in their teeth, lungs, skin, feet, and genital areas.

When neuropathy involves the bladder, infection accurs more frequently. It may make you unaware of the need to urinate, which can lead to a urinary tract infection. You may lose feeling in the arms, legs, or feet; a cut or burn will not cause pain and may not get treated. Neglect leads to infection.

Your legs and feet are targets for infections because

✦Neuropathy numbs legs and feet.

✦Injury opens the door to infection.

✦Diseased blood vessels restrict circulation to the legs and feet, impairing the healing process.

✦High blood glucose paralyses the body's defense cells (the white blood cells)

No matter where in the body it is—in gums, vagina, skin, or feet—an infection can be prevented or treated with better blood glucose control. You can also do other things to prevent some of the more common kinds of infections.

Prevention and Treatment

Bacteria adore the areas between your gums and teeth. Brush and floss daily to avoid periodontitis, otherwise known as gum disease. Have your teeth cleaned by a dentist every 6 months. If bacteria set in, they may destroy bone in your tooth socket and cause sores on your gums. Inflamed gums pull away from the teeth and jaw bone; bacteria will multiply in the gap. The teeth may even become loose and fall out. Depending on the severity, your dentist may need to scrape plaque from your teeth, remove dead tissue from around the tooth root, or perform surgery.

Women may get recurrent vaginal infections from the yeast *Candida*. High glucose levels combined with a moist environment make yeast infections likely. To help prevent them, wear only all-cotton underwear and avoid air-restricting pants and pantyhose. If you think you have a yeast infection, make sure your doctor agrees with your diagnosis before your treat it. You might confuse it with other conditions. After diagnosis, you probably can treat the yeast infection yourself with a nonprescription cream.

Your feet deserve special attention; no matter how much you weigh, they bear a heavy load. They are so vulnerable to neuropathy and injury that you need to check them every day for ulcers, calluses, corns and other visible problems. See your doctor if you have any concerns—especially if you find an ulcer. You can take action to prevent lower-limb infection. See Chapter 7, pages 136–137 (Go the Extra Mile for Your Feet) for some self-care tips for your feet.

To keep good blood flow to your feet, you should lower high blood pressure and cholesterol levels (with better food choices and medication if necessary) and take regular walks or get some form of sustained exercise daily. And again, try hard to quit smoking! Smokers account for 95% of all amputations.

If a lower-limb infection goes out of control, a surgeon may need to remove part of the foot or leg to save the rest of it from becoming infected. Amputation is frightening, but it does not mean the end of a normal lifestyle. It's not even the end of walking. The surgeon will remove as little of the limb as possible so that walking will be less difficult. After the limb heals, a prosthesis will be fitted. New prosthetic limbs are lighter and more comfortable than the clunky models of the past. Some have "spring" in the foot, hydraulic joints, and rotator units for twisting. Some even allow for running and jumping.

Diabetes and Sex

For Women

Sex should be as pleasurable for you as for any woman. Luckily, diabetes does not decrease sexual ability for women. Diabetes can create a few problems, but all are treatable. Like everything else about your health, your sex life can be improved by good blood glucose control. The fatigue that comes with high blood glucose levels can decrease your desire for sex. High blood glucose levels can also increase your chances of developing vaginal infections, such as recurrent yeast infections. Besides being painful, vaginal infections can make intercourse less desirable.

Sex can lower your blood glucose levels. Women who wear insulin pumps usually remove them during sex and don't miss the insulin at all. If you use injections, consider decreasing your presex dose or eat a little extra food. Self-monitoring will tell you how your body reacts to sexual excitement.

The most common sexual complaint of women with diabetes is decreased vaginal lubrication leading to painful intercourse. Ask your doctor if an over-the-counter lubrication jelly is right for you. In women past menopause, this problem is sometimes treated with estrogen.

Neuropathy can sometimes cause the nerves that supply the genital area to lose feeling. Reaching and maintaining good blood glucose control may help counteract this. You may also want to try vibrators or other forms of stimulation around the clitoris.

If neuropathy has affected your bladder to the extent that you involuntarily urinate during intercourse or orgasm, try urinating before and after sex. This is also a good rule of thumb to prevent urinary tract infections.

If you're on dialysis for end-stage renal disease, you may produce large amounts of the hormone prolactin, which decreases sexual desire. Be sure to discuss this with your kidney specialist or doctor.

For Men
A reported 10 million men in the general population

have experienced impotence, but the actual number may be much greater. Men who have diabetes have a special reason to learn about impotence, because it occurs among 50 to 60% of all men with diabetes who are over 50 years old. It can affect younger men, too.

Impotence may have more than 100 causes, some psychological, some biological. Psychological impotence has to do with the brain's lack of response to sexual stimulation. Biological impotence is related to physical causes and can involve hormones, the circulatory system, or the nervous system.

The most common causes of impotence in men with diabetes are diseases of the blood vessels and nerves. When the nerves are damaged, small blood vessels don't relax, which prevents them from expanding with the flow of blood that makes the penis erect. Tests for this consist of a mild electrical current that stimulates the nerves in the penis to measure their ability to respond.

Rarely, impotence occurs when blood vessels are blocked or made narrow because of vascular disease. One test for blood vessel damage measures the blood pressure in the penis and compares it to the blood pressure in the arm. Another test involves a shot of a drug or mixture of drugs into the penis. These drugs bypass nerves. If you then have an erection, damaged blood vessels are not the problem. If you don't have an erection or the response is limited, then the larger blood vessels may be blocked. Your doctor can use an ultrasound scanner or a process called *angiography* to find out if this blockage is the problem.

For about 10 to 15% of men with biological impotence, the cause is a lack of the male sex hormone testosterone. Your doctor can measure your testosterone level to find out if this is the problem.

Finally, some common drugs can affect the ability

to have an erection. Drugs used to treat hypertension, anxiety, depression, and peptic ulcers may cause impotence in some men but not in others. If you are having signs of impotence and take drugs for any of these conditions, let your doctor know.

If your impotence is psychologically rooted or if you have a fear of impotence that affects your sex life, you may want to ask your doctor to suggest a therapist who is experienced in helping people with sexual issues.

Although impotence may be difficult to talk about, discussing it with your doctor is important. For one thing, impotence is much more common than you think, and a frank conversation with your doctor will bring you that much closer to finding answers that can help you. You may need treatment by specialists, such as urologists, internists, psychiatrists, or psychologists. They can diagnose the cause of impotence and offer a range of treatment choices, including some that involve your sexual partner, if you are interested.

Prevention
Good blood glucose control is a safeguard against impotence. Good control will help you avoid the complications of diabetes that can cause impotence, such as nerve and blood vessel diseases.

Studies have shown that drinking excessive amounts of alcohol can contribute to impotence. Alcohol is directly toxic to nerves. Smoking, which may lead to vascular disease, should also be avoided.

Treatment
If your impotence has biological causes, a range of treatment choices is available. You can choose an option that suits your needs and desires and those of your partner.

Injection of certain drugs into the penis is one method of treating impotence. Generally, an erection brought about by injection lasts from 30 minutes to 1 hour. Side effects can include bruising and prolonged erection.

Another option is using a mechanical device that causes an erection. A vacuum device or vacuum pump is one such option. To use this device, a container is placed around the penis and a pump pulls air out of the container. The vacuum that is created pulls blood into the penis, producing an erection. To maintain the erection you remove the container and place a rubber band around the base of the penis. After 20 minutes, continuing to wear the rubber band can bruise the penis.

There are devices that can be surgically inserted into the penis. You should probably see a urologist with special knowledge about implants. Be sure to ask about the risk of infection or the need for further surgery if the device breaks or fails to work.

If a lack of testosterone is the cause of impotence, the hormone can be replaced through injections usually every 2 weeks or with a patch placed on the scrotum.

Because impotence can be the result of a mixture of causes, you may need several forms of therapy. Or, you may choose to have no treatment at all. These choices are personal, and any choice that answers your needs is valid.

Other Complications

You may also feel the impact of high blood glucose levels in your joints. If excess glucose attaches to tendons, your fingers and other bending points may lose flexibility. The tendons of the hand may tighten, causing the fingers to stiffen or curl inward. This limited joint mobility is not usually painful. (Pain is more common in carpal tunnel syndrome or other tendon problems.) But it is a sign that other tissues may also be damaged from excess blood glucose. Your doctor will check carefully for other complications and help you achieve better control.

An Idea of the Risk

Cardiovascular Disease

People with diabetes are...
*2 to 4 times more likely to get heart disease
*5 times more likely to have a stroke
than people without diabetes.

Cardiovascular disease causes more than half of the deaths in older people with diabetes.

Retinopathy

People with diabetes are...
*4 times more likely to become blind than people without diabetes.

After 5 years of living with type I diabetes, 13% of people have some type of retinopathy. After 15 years, 25% of people with type I diabetes have proliferative retinopathy. After 20 years, half have this complication. After 20 years, 95% have signs of retinopathy.

Nephropathy

People with diabetes are...
*20 times more likely to get end-stage renal disease than people without diabetes.

After 15 years of living with type I diabetes, one-third of people have kidney disease.

Neuropathy

After 25 years of living with diabetes, at least half of people have neuropathy. Autonomic neuropathy occurs in 20 to 40% of people with diabetes.

Infections

People with diabetes are...
*28 times more likely to have a lower-limb amputa tion than people without diabetes.
About 40% of people with type I diabetes older than 19 have gum disease.

Seven

Help With Good Health Care

Diabetes has its most noticeable effect on your blood glucose, but it can also affect the rest of you, from head to toe. That's why managing your diabetes means managing your total health care. These days, diabetes care is viewed as a team effort. You, your family and friends, doctors, nurse educators, dietitians, and other health-care professionals are key players on your **health-care team**.

You will spend time with these professionals writing a treatment plan that suits your unique needs. Your team can help you in the short term, when you have questions about your insulin, get sick, or need to change your diet. They can also help you over the long term, by working to prevent complications of diabetes such as eye disease, heart disease, nerve damage, and kidney disease.

Team Captain

You are the captain of your health-care team. You decide when to exercise, you decide what and how much to eat, you take your medications, and you monitor the results. You are the first to notice any problems. Listen to your body. The other team members rely on you to tell them what you have learned about your body and its responses to diabetes.

As team captain, you are responsible for picking the other players on your team. Be sure to remember your support system—family or friends who can help you with your daily routine and with emergencies. Then think of your *primary-care doctor*, the doctor you see for general check-ups and when you are sick. Ask your primary-care doctor to be your co-captain, in charge of giving the other health-care professionals information about your health and diabetes control.

Finding Dr. Right

Just two months before she was ready to fly across the country to graduate school, Andrea learned she had type I diabetes. Everything was new to her—blood glucose tests, insulin shots, and a carefully controlled diet. And moving to a new state meant choosing a new doctor too. Armed with a few references from her family doctor, Andrea started looking.

Andrea knew she would see her primary-care doctor at least every 3 months, and much more often while she was still getting her diabetes under control. She planned to interview any doctor she was considering. She made a list of her four biggest concerns in finding Dr. Right.

❖Most importantly, Andrea wanted someone who would value open and clear communication. The doctor should listen to her questions and concerns and should tailor medical care to her unique needs. The right doctor would take time to fully explain hard terms and concepts.

❖Ideally, Dr. Right would be an endocrinologist. Endocrinologists have thoroughly studied diabetes and other conditions that affect hormones. If she couldn't find an endocrinologist nearby, Andrea planned to look for a family practice doctor or an internist with expertise in caring for people with diabetes.

❖If possible, Dr. Right would be covered by Andrea's health insurance plan. Some plans will completely cover your costs only if you see a physician on their list of "preferred" providers. (You need to know the ground rules for your plan. See Chapter 12 for more information on insurance.)

❖Also, if possible, Dr. Right would agree to be a team player. He or she would coordinate Andrea's medical care by talking to the other members of her health-care team about how her diabetes control was working. She planned to ask whether the physician would charge extra consultation costs for this approach.

Your Primary-Care Physician's Job

Whether you're a newly diagnosed patient like Andrea, or a veteran of diabetes treatment, you should receive certain basic care from your doctor.

A complete physical exam once a year. A good physical exam starts out with a talk between you and the doctor. She or he will probably look over your blood glucose measurements and discuss your insulin therapy or other medications. You can give the doctor an update on any lifestyle changes you are making, such as quitting smoking or starting exercise. You may ask whether it's time to consult with one or more of the other professionals on your team. Speak up—ask questions and talk about the parts of your treatment plan that are working and those that are not.

A good physical exam also involves a close look at all the parts of your body, from head to toe. The doctor is trained to discover small problems and help prevent them from becoming larger ones. She or he will examine all of the following (and maybe more):

❖**Total body weight**: Talk to the doctor about the body weight you think is best for you.

❖**Blood pressure and pulse**: Ask your doctor to

tell you your current blood pressure and pulse and what levels are best for you to achieve. Also ask about your target heart rate for exercise.

✦**Eyes**: Your primary-care physician will check your eyes for problems and ask about any changes in your vision.

✦**Heart and lungs**: This check is usually done by listening to your heart and lungs through a stethoscope. An electrocardiogram or even a stress electrocardiogram may be needed to detect symptom-free heart disease. These tests monitor the electrical activity and the pumping of your heart muscle.

✦**Feet**: Remove your shoes and socks to remind your doctor to look at your feet each time you visit, not just during complete physicals. They should be checked for pulses, reflexes, calluses, infections, and sores. They will also be examined for loss of pain or feeling, and the prickly sensation that can mean neuropathy.

✦**Skin**: Your largest organ, your skin, will be examined by sight, with special attention to insulin injection sites.

✦**Nervous system**: This will be examined by testing your reflexes and your ability to feel sharpness of a pin or the light touch of cotton or a brush. Bring up any persistent problems like dizziness on standing; pain, burning sensation, or numbness in your legs or arms; constipation or diarrhea; difficulty urinating; or difficulty with erection or sexual satisfaction.

✦**Mouth and neck**: This includes examining your gums, teeth, mouth, and throat; feeling for swelling in the glands in your neck; and asking about your brushing and flossing habits. Ask your doctor about your thyroid gland, located in your neck. At your initial physical exam after diagnosis of your diabetes, thyroid function tests should be performed.

✦**Blood**: A sample of blood will be taken to examine the levels of glucose and glycated hemoglobin. A fasting lipid profile, which measures cholesterol and triglycerides, will determine the levels of these fats in your blood. The doctor will also assess how well your kidneys are working by testing for urea nitrogen and serum creatinine.

✦**Urine**: Testing urine also helps your doctor check your kidney function. Your urine should be tested for ketones, glucose, and protein. People with diabetes are more likely to have infections of the urinary tract because of the high amount of glucose in the urine and the loss of the sensation of knowing when the bladder is full or empty due to neuropathy. A urine culture may be needed if you have symptoms of infection.

✦**Preventive vaccinations**: People with diabetes are more likely to get complications from the flu or pneumonia. Ask about vaccines to prevent these conditions.

✦**Other**: These may be done by a doctor other than your primary care physician. For women, tests should also include a Pap smear, mammogram, and a gynecological and rectal exam. Use of contraceptives and plans for pregnancy should be discussed. Men should receive prostate and rectal exams. In both men and women, stool specimens can be tested for blood.

✦**Specific problems**: Your doctor should ask you to explain anything unusual you've noticed or any concerns you have; for example, a sore shoulder or abdominal pain. Don't be afraid to bring up sexual or other personal topics.

A glycated hemoglobin check every 3 months. This blood test will tell your doctor how well, on average, your blood glucose control has worked over the past 3 months. Your doctor should check the results of this test against your own self-monitoring records.

When you're under the weather. Talk to your doctor about sick days. What symptoms are serious enough that you need to call the doctor? (See "Chicken Soup and Lots of Liquids" below.)

As needed. Many changes in your health might bring you back to your doctor much more often than every 3 months. Maybe you're just starting insulin, or you're changing your dose and your blood glucose is not in control. Perhaps you and your doctor are finding a way to control your high blood pressure. You might visit as often as every day until your routine begins to work.

The Rest of the Team

Diabetes is a complicated disease, and you may gain from the skill of other health professionals working with your primary-care physician. The team approach acknowledges that diabetes affects many aspects of your life each day. You can't learn all you need to know during a 1-hour visit with your doctor. Talk to your primary-care doctor about recruiting the rest of your health-care team. Your doctor or your local American Diabetes Association chapter may be able to recommend qualified people. Be sure that each team member has phone and fax numbers for the rest of the team so that they can communicate about changes in your control or care.

Your Diabetes Educator

Ron took his insulin faithfully every day—a shot before breakfast and another in the evening. His glucose was near ideal levels, but Ron had begun to notice tough lumps all around the injection site on his abdomen. His primary-care physician recommended a meeting with a nurse educator or diabetes nurse practitioner to work on improving site rotation.

You may want to use the services of a nurse educator or diabetes nurse practitioner, a registered nurse (RN) with special training and experience in caring for people with diabetes. The initials CDE (certified diabetes educator) indicate that a nurse or a dietitian has passed a national qualifying exam in diabetes education and is up-to-date about diabetes care. You may find such a nurse in the offices of doctors who treat many patients with diabetes. The American Association of Diabetes Educators can also provide local referrals (See Resources, page 260).

Diabetes education programs. You can learn one-on-one or with others through a diabetes education program. The American Diabetes Association affiliate in your state can refer you to a program that has been recognized as meeting National Standards. Education programs that meet the National Standards should be able to cover all of the following topics:

◆General facts about diabetes including what causes it;

◆Adjusting psychologically to caring for your diabetes and teaching others;

◆Using your family or friends for support;

◆Understanding your eating plan and the importance of matching your insulin amount to your meal portions;

◆Exercising wisely to manage blood glucose and avoid hypoglycemia;

◆Taking medications such as insulin effectively;

◆Balancing nutrition, exercise, and insulin;

◆Testing your blood glucose accurately and recording it properly;

◆Dealing with hyperglycemia and hypoglycemia — their symptoms, causes, and treatments;

◆Handling minor illnesses;

◆Preventing or treating long-term complications;

✦Maintaining good hygiene including skin, foot, and dental care;

✦Weighing the benefits and responsibilities of care, avoiding complications, and understanding the impact of smoking and alcohol on diabetes;

✦Using the health-care system, including your health-care team, to help you take care of your diabetes; and

✦Finding community resources for help with all aspects of diabetes.

Be sure that the program's staff writes to inform your physician of what you did in the program.

Your Dietitian

Three years after Marie had been diagnosed with diabetes, she visited her dietitian. Her blood glucose levels had been getting higher over the last few months, and she'd just read an article about neuropathy. She thought that an adjustment in what she was eating and when she ate might help her keep the blood glucose levels closer to normal throughout the day. Close to normal blood glucose levels might help her prevent the painful symptoms of neuropathy, too.

The nurse pumped the blood pressure cuff tight, and Charles gritted his teeth. When he heard the two numbers, he knew his blood pressure was too high. The doctor advised him to exercise, lose weight, and eat a low-sodium diet to help reduce hypertension. Charles decided to see his dietitian about how to cut his sodium without losing the foods he loved.

A registered dietitian (RD) is a health-care professional with training and expertise in the field of food and nutrition. It's a good idea to see a dietitian for a diet assessment every 6 months to 1 year. A dietitian helps you understand the role of nutrition in your management plan and develop a dietary strategy—a crucial component to living well with diabetes. Your meal plan can be adapted to special goals such as weight loss or reducing dietary fat and sodium, and also to your likes and dislikes ,work schedule, and lifestyle.

Does your meal plan need a change? If you answer yes to any of the following questions, then it's time your meal plan was brought up-to-date.

✦Has your meal plan been reviewed in the last year?

✦Is your diabetes or body weight more difficult to control than usual?

✦Are you bored with your meals?

✦Have you started an exercise program or changed your insulin regimen since your last diet check-up?

✦Are you concerned about preventing or have you been diagnosed with high blood pressure, high cholesterol levels, or kidney disease?

Look for the initials RD (registered dietitian), which tell you that the dietitian has passed a national credentialing exam. Many states also require a license, so you'll often see the initials LD (licensed dietitian). Some dietitians are also CDEs. The American Dietetic Association can recommend qualified dietitians in your area (See Resources, page 260). Other good sources of recommendations are your primary-care physician, area hospitals, and your local American Diabetes Association chapter.

An assessment visit generally takes an hour to an hour and a half. Follow-up visits run about 30 minutes. Follow-up visits allow for sharing further helpful information, progress checks, and adjustments to your meal plan.

Dietitians teach you many useful skills: how to use *Exchange Lists for Meal Planning*, published by the American Diabetes Association and the American Dietetic Association; how to count dietary carbohydrate or fat and make adjustments in your insulin dose; how to read food labels; how to handle eating out in restaurants; and how to make healthy food choices when grocery shopping. Dietitians help you discover a range of nutritional resources, including cookbooks and reference materials, so you can learn how to prepare healthy, delicious, and satisfying meals. They can help you add spice to your life by showing you how to maintain good blood glucose control even if you eat in ethnic restaurants, throw a party, or eat a Thanksgiving feast earlier than you normally would eat dinner.

Your Exercise Physiologist

Almost every time she exercised, Terry felt the classic signs of a hypoglycemic reaction. Her heart pounded, she began to sweat, her body grew shaky, and she grew exasperated. Exercise should be good for her, she thought, not make her feel awful. Terry's family doctor referred her to an exercise physiologist with experience in diabetes care. With his help, she learned to estimate how long she could exercise based on her preexercise glucose level and when to eat snacks. She learned what foods to eat if her blood glucose levels were low hours after exercise.

Like Terry, you know you have to exercise. But do you know how? Fitness programs are best designed by a person trained in the scientific basis of exercise and in safe conditioning. Look for someone with a master's or doctoral degree in exercise physiology or a licensed health-care professional with graduate training in this area. You may want someone certified by the American College of Sports Medicine (See Resources, page 264).

Exercise physiologists can help you select proper exercises, set realistic goals, or stay motivated and disciplined in your exercise routine. They can tailor programs to your health needs. You may want to improve your cardiovascular fitness, lower your blood glucose, lose weight, or develop muscle strength and flexibility. Special exercise programs help you work out even if you are overweight, have been inactive for a long time, or have arthritis. You should have your primary-care physician approve any exercise program you select.

Your Mental Health Counselor

Shelly, a middle-aged woman with type I diabetes, prides herself on her discipline in her self-care. Her blood glucose is well under control. So whenever Shelly finds her blood glucose level a bit higher than she wants to see it, she feels like a failure. Her self-blame makes it hard for her to work for the rest of the day. She mopes around and thinks, "I can't do anything right."

Diabetes brings its share of stresses to your thoughts and feelings, not just your body. Shelly probably would benefit from seeing a therapist, such as a social worker, family therapist, psychologist, or psychiatrist. This person could help her deal with the personal and emotional aspects of diabetes.

✦**A social worker** should have a master's degree in social work, known as an MSW, as well as training in individual, group, and family therapy. Social workers can help you cope with many issues relating to diabetes control, from problems in the family or in work situations to locating resources to help with medical or financial needs.

✦**A marriage and family therapist** should have a master's degree in a mental health field and added training in individual, family, and marriage therapy. These therapists can help you with personal difficulties in your family, your marriage, or your job.

✦**A clinical psychologist** has a master's or doctoral degree in psychology and is trained in individual, group, and family psychology. You might visit a psychologist during a particularly stressful few weeks or months or on a long-term basis to work out more deep-seated problems.

✦A **psychiatrist** is a doctor with the medical training to understand how the physical aspects of diabetes can contribute to your psychological health. A psychiatrist can also prescribe medications or hospitalization for emotional problems when needed.

Your Eye Doctor

George first saw spots at the company softball game. He stepped up to bat, looked toward the pitcher, and couldn't focus on the ball at all. All he saw were strange blotches dancing around his field of vision. With this warning sign, he made an appointment for an eye exam.

Look out for your eyes. Good preventive care can ward off some of the long-term complications of diabetes and keep your vision clear. A professional eye exam reveals whether there have been changes in the tiny blood vessels that supply your retinas (the "screens" at the back of your eyes that receive visual images). These changes could be an early sign of diabetic retinopathy, which can lead to blindness if not treated.

Your primary-care physician will look into your eyes during your yearly physical exams, but you also need the more thorough exam of an eye doctor. If you are over 30 years old when you are diagnosed with diabetes, or if you are between 12 and 30 years old and have had diabetes for at least 5 years, you need a comprehensive eye and visual exam by an eye doctor every year. Also have an examination if you notice changes in your vision or if you are pregnant or planning a pregnancy (See an ophthalmologist during the first trimester).

Ophthalmologists are medical doctors who can treat eye problems both medically and surgically. **Retina specialists** are ophthalmologists with further training in the diagnosis and treatment of diseases of the retina. **Optometrists** are trained in examining the eye for certain problems, such as how well your eyes focus. They are not medical doctors and are not able to prescribe medications in some states.

You should see an ophthalmologist if you, your family doctor, or your optometrist notice any of the following signs:

✦unexplained visual problems (spots, "floaters," or cobwebs in your field of vision; blurred or distorted vision; blind spots; eye pain or persistent redness).

✦loss of your ability to read books or traffic signs, or to distinguish familiar objects.

✦increased pressure within the eye (a warning sign of glaucoma). Some internal medicine and family doctors and most optometrists test for this.

✦any abnormality of the retina. Internists, family practitioners, and optometrists should test for this but should refer retinal problems to ophthalmologists.

✦retinopathy, the leaking of blood vessels that supply the retina, is the main cause of blindness in people with diabetes.

Your Podiatrist

Hopping out of the shower, Norma grabbed her towel and began drying her feet. "Weird," she thought, "a sore on the ball of my foot. I didn't even feel it." A visit to the podiatrist confirmed that Norma had a foot ulcer, caught early enough to be easily treated.

People with diabetes can develop poor blood flow and nerve damage in their feet. Sores, even small ones, can quickly turn into serious problems. Check your feet daily. Your primary-care physician may refer you to a podiatrist. Podiatrists graduate from a college of podiatry with a Doctor of Podiatric Medicine (DPM) degree. They have completed residencies in podiatry and can do surgery and prescribe medicine for your feet (See Resources, page 261).

Your Dermatologist

Ricardo's skin felt so dry he might as well live in a desert, he thought. His feet cracked and peeled, too. Lotion gave him little relief. Ricardo's doctor suggested a visit to a dermatologist to find the best solution to his very dry skin.

Overly dry skin is a common companion to poor diabetes control and diabetic neuropathy. Water is lost when the body produces extra urine to rid itself of excess blood glucose. The dehydration leads to dry skin.

The skin is also a tempting target for infections, and having diabetes raises your risk of skin infections—on your feet and all over. If your blood glucose is not well controlled, skin infections are even more likely. Good skin care and blood glucose control can steer you clear of most infections (see "Save Your Skin" below). If you do find an area infected, you may want to see a dermatologist. Dermatologists are medical doctors with specialized training in skin disorders.

Your Dentist

Natasha hated flossing her teeth, but she'd managed to ignore the boring nightly routine for a few years now. She brushed of course, right after her insulin shot. She figured that would get rid of the plaque on her teeth. But something told her she ought to pick up the floss again; her gums began to bleed almost every time she brushed her teeth. A trip to the dentist showed mild gingivitis, or gum disease.

Just like people, bacteria love sweets. When you have high glucose levels, your saliva makes your mouth a home for the bacteria that cause gum infection. And diabetes can also make it harder for your mouth to fight infections once they start.

To dodge gum disease, get your teeth cleaned by the dentist every 6 months. Tell the dentist you have diabetes, and ask the dentist or dental hygienist to okay your brushing and flossing technique. Beyond regular visits, you should call the dentist if you notice any signs of gum disease. (See "Watch Your Mouth" below for warning signs.)

Checking Your Body

You won't spend every day at the doctor's office, but every day should include a routine of self-care. Take preventive steps, care for small problems, and know when to call the doctor. Follow these checklists for quick self-care. It's as easy as brushing your teeth.

Watch Your Mouth

Left uncontrolled, diabetes can cause severe gum disease and abscesses in young and old. So keep monitoring your blood glucose.

1. ___ Brush at least twice a day to fight plaque. Use a soft nylon brush with rounded ends on the bristles. Tilt the bristles at about a 45-degree angle against the gum line and brush gently in a scrubbing motion. Brush front and back, and also brush the chewing surfaces.

2. ___ Brush the rough upper surface of the tongue.

3. ___ Use dental floss once a day to remove bacteria from between your teeth. Special floss holders and various types of floss are available to make flossing easier.

4. ___ Have your teeth cleaned and checked by the dentist at least every 6 months.

5. ___ Call your dentist if you find:

✦Your gums bleed when you brush or eat.

✦Your gums are red, swollen, or tender.

✦Your gums have pulled away from your teeth.

✦Pus appears between your teeth and gums when the gums are touched.

✦Your teeth are becoming loose or changing position.

✦Any change in the way dentures or partial plates fit.

✦Any change in the way your teeth fit together when you bite.

✦Persistent bad breath or bad taste in your mouth.

Go the Extra Mile for Your Feet

1. ___ Wash your feet every day with a mild soap. Dry them off carefully, especially between the toes. If your feet are dry, apply a thin lubricant or cream everywhere except between the toes (to avoid athlete's foot).

2. ___ Inspect your feet and between your toes daily. You can use a mirror to see the bottoms of your feet. If your vision is impaired, have a family member examine your feet. Look for:

    a. ___ swollen areas

    b. ___ red areas

    c. ___ any breaks, cuts, or scratches

    d. ___ patches of dry skin

    e. ___ very cold areas (could mean poor circulation)

    f. ___ very warm areas (could mean an infection)

3. ___ Never go barefoot, because you may not feel it if you step on something. Aqua socks for ocean and pool use are now popular with everyone.

4. ___ Be careful when you trim your toenails. Cut your nails straight across. If they are very thick and curved or if your sight is not adequate, you may need professional help to cut them properly.

5. ___ Make sure you have comfortable, well-fitting shoes, made of leather. Do not expect to "break in" new shoes. Make sure there is nothing in the shoe that will rub against your foot, such as a pebble. If you have recurring problems, you may need special therapeutic foot wear. If you have neuropathy, you may not be able to rely on how a shoe feels for fit. Consult a prescription footwear specialist (See Resources, page 262).

6. ___ Change your socks or stockings every day. Socks or stockings should be even and smooth.

7. ___ Never use a heating pad, a hot-water bottle, or a hot-water soak on your feet—you may not feel a burn.

8. ___ Follow commonsense guidelines in caring for your feet (Table 1). Never try amateur surgery on corns or calluses—get them professionally treated.

9. ___ Call your doctor, who may refer you to a podiatrist, if you have

  ✦an ulcer or open sore on your foot.
  ✦any infection in a cut or blister.
  ✦a red, tender toe—possibly an ingrown toenail.
  ✦any change in feeling such as pain, tingling, numbness, or burning.
  ✦any change in how your foot looks—possibly a plantar wart or change in circulation.
  ✦any puncture wound (for example, if you step on a nail or thorn).

Save Your Skin

Keeping your blood glucose in check will help keep your body hydrated and prevent very dry skin. You will lose less fluid in your urine if your body has less extra glucose to flush out. Skin infections are also less likely if your diabetes is well controlled.

1. ___ Keep your skin clean. If you have dry skin, use a superfatted soap such as Dove, Basis, Keri, or Oilatum.

Table 1. Caring for Common Foot Problems

If you have....	You should...
Cuts or cracks in your skin	Keep the area clean and dry to avoid infections.
Dry, scaly skin	Apply a thin coating of lubricant twice a day, everywhere except between the toes.
Calluses	Use a pumice stone gently each day. Never try to cut calluses out yourself. You may want to try shoe inserts to avoid them.
Foot ulcers	Get immediate medical attention, and stay off your foot.
Neuropathy	Inspect your feet every day. Never walk barefoot or use your feet to test the temperature of bath water.
Poor circulation (cold feet, leg cramps, dry or shiny skin)	Wear warm socks, even in bed. Use an electric blanket to warm your bed, but turn it off before you get in. Don't use heating pads or hot water bottles, and never soak your feet in hot water. Avoid smoking, sitting with your legs crossed, and wearing garters or tight socks.

2. ___ Dry off well after washing. Be sure to prevent moisture in the folds of the skin, such as in the groin, between the toes, and under the breasts and armpits where fungal infections can occur. Try using talcum powder.

3. ___ Avoid very hot baths and showers because you can burn your skin without realizing what's happening if you have neuropathy, or nerve damage.

4. ___ Prevent dry skin. When you scratch dry, itchy skin, you can break the skin and open the door to bacteria. After you dry off from a shower, you may need an oil-in-water skin cream such as Lubriderm or Alpha-Keri. On cold and windy days, you may need to moisturize often to prevent chapping.

5. ___ Use mild shampoos. Don't use feminine hygiene sprays. Wear all-cotton underwear and socks, which allow air to circulate better than other types.

6. ___ Treat cuts quickly. For minor cuts, clean the area with soap, water, and hydrogen peroxide. Then, lightly dress with a Telfa pad wrapped with a knot of gauze or secured with paper tape. **DO NOT** use antiseptics such as Mercurochrome, alcohol, or iodine because they irritate the skin. Only use antibiotic creams and ointments for a few days without consulting your physician.

7. ___ Drink lots of water (unless your doctor advises otherwise).

8. ___ Call your doctor if

✦you have the redness, swelling, pus, or pain that might indicate a bacterial infection

✦you have jock itch, athlete's foot, ringworm, vaginal itching, or other signs of a fungal infection

✦blisters or bumps appear anywhere, especially on the backs of your fingers, hands, toes, arms, legs, or buttocks. These are a signal of poor glucose control.

✦Rashes, bumps, or pits crop up near insulin injection sites.

A reddish-yellow rash known as diabetic dermopathy may appear on the lower legs and shins. It does not hurt, ulcerate, or itch. It does not require treatment, but it does show that the small blood vessels are changing. If you develop larger, itchy, painful or ulcerated patches, you should call your doctor.

You've Got Two Eyes...

Take care of your eyes by keeping your diabetes controlled and visiting your eye doctor yearly.

1. ___ Have a thorough eye exam at the time of diabetes diagnosis if you are over 30 and yearly thereafter. If you are between 12 and 30 and have had diabetes for at least 5 years, also have a comprehensive exam yearly.

2. ___ After the initial exam, see an eye doctor familiar with retinopathy and other diabetes complications once a year.

3. ___ Call your primary-care doctor if you notice changes in your vision, but don't panic. Highs and lows in your blood glucose may cause temporary blurring in your vision.

4. ___ Keep your blood glucose levels under control. You will help prevent damage to the small blood vessels that run through your retina.

5. ___ Have regular blood pressure checks, and work to keep your blood pressure in the healthy range.

6. ___ Discuss your exercise program with your eye doctor. Some activities can raise the pressure inside your eyes and lead to bleeding in the retina.

7. ___ If you have retinopathy, avoid taking birth control pills because they may affect the clotting of your blood or increase your blood pressure.

Chicken Soup and Lots of Liquids

Being sick is no fun for anyone. But it poses special

problems for your diabetes care. Vomiting or loss of appetite can affect your diabetes control and lead to dehydration. Sickness also raises your blood glucose. To deal with the stress of illness, your body releases hormones that normally help the body fight disease. Unfortunately, these hormones also elevate blood glucose levels and counteract the glucose-lowering effects of insulin. You can even develop ketoacidosis, a poisoning of the blood with ketones that leads to diabetic coma.

You, your primary-care physician, and your diabetes educator or dietitian can work out a plan to prepare for common illnesses such as colds and flu before they strike.

Write down a plan of action that includes when to call the doctor, how often to test your blood and urine, whether to change your insulin, and what foods and fluids to take during your illness. At the first sign of illness, test your glucose and be prepared to follow your sick-day plan.

Besides watching game shows on the couch, you should...

1. ___ Always take your normal dose of insulin—even if you can't eat. Your doctor may even prescribe more insulin to counteract the excess glucose that your body releases when you are sick. You and your doctor should agree on what blood glucose levels call for you to change your dose.

2. ___ Monitor your blood glucose and ketone levels about every 4 hours. If the levels are high or you are pregnant, you may need to monitor more often.

3. ___ Substitute sick-day foods for normal foods if nausea or vomiting make it difficult to eat (Table 2).

4. ___ Drink plenty of caffeine-free liquids. If you are losing fluids by vomiting, fever, or diarrhea, you may need nondiet soft drinks or sports drinks with sugar or carbohydrate. This can help prevent the hypo-

glycemia caused by not eating or taking extra insulin. If vomiting or diarrhea are intense, try drinking 3 to 6 ounces an hour to keep blood glucose stable.

Be prepared for under-the-weather days with the following steps:

1. ___ Talk to your dietitian about which sick-day foods will cover your basic eating plan. Prepare a sick-day meal plan before you ever become ill. Keep on hand the mild foods you could eat and drink, such as diet and regular soft drinks, chicken soup, bouillon cubes, broth, applesauce, and gelatin.

2. ___ Keep on hand a fever thermometer and a small supply of common sick-day medications that have been approved by your doctor.

Some medications sold over the counter are not recommended for people with diabetes. Cough and cold medications labeled "decongestants" contain compounds (such as pseudoephedrine) that can raise blood glucose level and blood pressure. As the packages say, do not take them without a doctor's advice. On the other hand, antihistamines are usually safe for people with diabetes without a doctor's order.

Many cough and cold remedies contain sugar and alcohol. You can try to find sugar-free preparations. A small amount of sugar is probably fine, as long as you realize you are taking it. Alcohol is a common component in nighttime cold medications such as Nyquil. Be sure you have eaten something before you take a medication with alcohol, or your blood glucose level may fall.

Pain medications are also usually safe in small doses. An occasional aspirin for a headache or for temporary fever control is not a problem. However, long-term use of aspirin for chronic pain control may lower your blood glucose level. Ibuprofen is not safe for people with kidney disease unless a doctor advises it. This drug could cause acute renal failure in people with kidney problems.

You may need to call your doctor if:

1. ___ An illness has continued for one or two days without improvement.

2. ___ Vomiting or diarrhea has continued for longer than 6 hours.

3. ___ Self-testing shows moderate to large amounts of ketones in your urine.

4. ___ Your blood glucose levels are outside your limits. For example, your blood glucose is over 240 mg/dl after taking two or three supplemental doses of Regular insulin as prearranged with your doctor, or your blood glucose is below 60 mg/dl.

5. ___ You have signs of extreme hyperglycemia (for example, very dry mouth or fruity odor to the breath), dehydration, or loss of mental competence.

6. ___ You are sleepier than is normal for you, even when ill.

7. ___ You have any stomach or chest pain or any difficulty breathing.

8. ___ You have any doubts about what you need to do for your illness.

Discuss this list with your doctor to see whether you need to add or subtract from it.

Table 2. Servings for Sick Days

One serving of **STARCH/BREAD**
1/2 cup mashed potatoes
1/3 cup cooked rice
6 saltine crackers
1/3 cup sugar-free frozen yogurt
1/4 cup sherbet
1 cup soup with rice or noodles
1 cup creamed soup (also 1 fat)
1/2 cup sugar-free pudding

One serving of **FRUIT**
1/2 cup applesauce
1/2 cup low-sugar
canned fruit
1 frozen fruit juice bar
1/2 cup fruit juice

One serving of **VEGETABLES**
1/2 cup well-cooked vegetables
(carrots or baby food veggies)
1/2 cup vegetable juice

One serving of **MEAT**
1/2 cup cottage cheese
1 ounce cheese
1 scrambled egg
1/2 cup egg substitute
4 ounces tofu

One serving of **MILK**
1/2 cup baked custard
8 oz. plain yogurt
1 cup low-fat milk

Eight

Healthy Food Choices

Foods on a diabetes meal plan are the same ones that are ideal for everyone. A healthy eating plan should make controlling blood glucose easier, not harder. A helpful plan:

◆Includes foods you like.

◆Takes your daily schedule into account and is flexible.

◆Helps keep blood glucose levels within your goal range.

◆Helps you reach and keep a healthy weight.

◆Helps prevent diet-related diseases like certain cancers and heart disease.

All that most people know about food and diabetes is, "Don't eat sugar." But, that's not the important thing. Instead, looking at how different foods affect your blood glucose levels will help you make decisions about which and how much of them to eat and when. Every time you check your blood glucose after a meal you learn more about how food affects your blood glucose level. This information helps you match your food to your activities and insulin dose.

Variety Adds More Than Spice

If you do only one thing for your good health each day, let it be eating a variety of foods. No one food can provide all the nutrients your body needs. Your body needs to replace parts (like muscle cells and blood), repair damage, and just keep you rolling along. To do this, it must have sources of the three important nutrients: carbohydrate, protein, and fat, as well as minerals and vitamins. Nature combines these nutrients in foods so your body can best use them. That's why eating a variety of foods is better than eating vitamin and mineral supplements.

Cereals, grains, pasta, bread, fruit, vegetables, legumes, and milk products are carbohydrate sources. Protein is found in meat, milk products, eggs, and fish, but there is a small amount in grains, bread, legumes, nuts, and vegetables. Fat is found in meat, milk products, oils, and nuts.

Calories are a measure of the energy provided by foods. Carbohydrates and proteins provide about the same amount of energy, 4 calories per gram. All fats provide more than twice that amount, 9 calories per gram. Thus, too many high-fat foods can make you put on excess weight and may increase your risk of heart disease. Make low-fat carbohydrates the mainstay of your meals. You need much less protein, and even less fat in your daily diet. It may help to see your eating plan as The Food Guide Pyramid. Eat tiny amounts of the foods near the top, and choose most of your foods from the carbohydrates, vegetables, and fruits from the base of the pyramid.

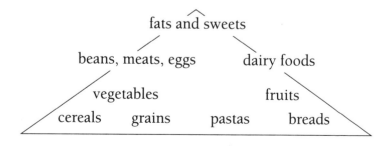

Carbohydrates

The carbohydrates you are encouraged to eat are dried beans, peas, and lentils; brown rice; and whole-grain flours, breads, crackers, and cereals. With these, you get the most nutrients for each calorie.

Sugars are also carbohydrates. Despite bad press, they really aren't off limits to people with diabetes. There is no evidence that people with diabetes should avoid sugars in favor of other foods that also contain carbohydrate.

We now know that the structure of the carbohydrate—simple versus complex—does not determine its effect on blood glucose levels. How much you eat, how quickly you eat, the way the food has been prepared, and the combination of foods eaten are what determine how quickly food is digested and absorbed. For instance, eating foods containing fat slows down their absorption.

So, your first priority should be to think about your *total carbohydrate intake* and how it changes your blood glucose level. If you aim to eat a certain total number of carbohydrates each day, and you eat a lot of sugary foods, you'll only get to eat a few of the more nutrient-rich starchy foods.

Calorie-free sugar substitutes do not raise your blood glucose levels. These include artificial sweeteners such as aspartame, acesulfame-K, and saccharin. Sugar alcohols, such as sorbitol, mannitol, and xylitol, have calories and are absorbed into the blood more slowly than glucose and usually cause less of a rise in blood glucose levels than glucose or sucrose. When consumed in large quantities (more than 20–50 grams, or 2/3–1 2/3 ounces in one day), sugar alcohols can cause intestinal distress and diarrhea.

You should be aware that many products that

have low-calorie sweeteners in them, such as diet desserts, often contain starches, other sugars, fats, and proteins, which can cause blood glucose levels to rise. So be sure to check the ingredients list to find out what you're eating.

Maltodextrin and polydextrose found in products such as sugar-free, nonfat yogurt, are bulking agents. Maltodextrin is a glucose syrup used to replace fat that has 4 calories per gram. Polydextrose is a partial substitute for sugar and fat. Most of it passes through the body, so it only has 1 calorie per gram. For people with diabetes there is no evidence that these nutritive sweeteners have any advantages over sugar in terms of calories or blood glucose response.

Protein

Proteins make replacement parts for our bodies and are not used for energy unless there are not enough carbohydrates and fats in the body. Protein is essential to good health, but Americans tend to eat more protein than is necessary. People who have kidney disease, nephropathy, may be advised to moderately limit their protein intake.

Meat, poultry, milk products, and eggs are sources of high-quality protein, but they come with cholesterol and saturated fat. Seafood is often a wise choice, because most varieties are lower in saturated fat and cholesterol than meat. A 3-ounce serving of shrimp, which has the highest cholesterol of commonly eaten shellfish, contains almost as much cholesterol as an egg yolk but has so little saturated fat that the cholesterol can't get into the blood.

Protein also comes from nuts, legumes, grains, and vegetables. Nuts are a high-fat source of protein, but vegetables, grains, and legumes are low in fat and saturated fat, contain no cholesterol, and have other nutrients as well. For example, a 1/3 cup serving of cooked beans has 3 grams of protein, as does 1/2 cup of corn (1 Starch/Bread Exchange). One cup of raw non-starchy vegetables or 1/2 cup of cooked non-starchy vegetables, such as carrots, onion, broccoli, or zucchini, gives you 2 grams of protein (1 Vegetable Exchange).

You can reduce the fat in meat by

✦broiling, roasting, grilling, or poaching rather than frying.

✦cutting off all visible fat before or after cooking and removing the skin from chicken and turkey.

✦chilling meat broth and drippings so the fat rises and solidifies so it can be skimmed off the top before making gravy or serving. You can also use this method to remove extra fat from canned broths and soups.

✦asking your butcher to tenderize lean cuts of meat through mechanical means without any chemical additives.

✦trying quick-cooking techniques such as stir-frying or grilling meat that you have marinated (in tiny amounts of oil or dressing with lots of seasonings) to enhance juiciness and flavor.

✦Steaming, poaching, or grilling fish.

Fats and Cholesterol

Although fat is an important part of a healthy diet, many Americans get too much saturated fat. Extra fat can clog up blood vessels and increase your chances of getting heart disease, some cancers, and stroke. So, you would be wise to limit the quantities of fat, especially saturated fat, and cholesterol that you eat each day.

Both the cholesterol and saturated fats found in food raise cholesterol in the blood. However, choosing leaner meats doesn't necessarily reduce the cholesterol. For instance, if you eat lean beef and pork, you will reduce the saturated fats but the cholesterol level is about the same. But if you choose low-fat or nonfat milk products, you can really cut down on your cholesterol intake. That's why skim milk and low-fat cheeses are good choices. It might help you to remember that only animal products contain cholesterol.

If you're counting, limit your dietary cholesterol to 300 milligrams a day and total fat to less than 30% of the calories (with saturated fats under 10%) a day. If you go over this one day, go under on others. To figure a rough estimate of how much fat you want to eat, decide on the number of calories you'll eat each day. Drop the last number (1200 becomes 120). Divide by 3. The answer is the number of grams of fat you can eat each day and meet the 30% of calories from fat guideline.

The Nutrition Facts section on food labels tells you how much fat, saturated fat, and calories from fat are in one serving. At the end of the day, or when figuring the meals to eat for the day, add up all the calories from fat from the labels on the foods you've eaten and any other hidden fats in foods without labels. This gives you the total of daily calories from fat. Divide that number by the total calories you've eaten for the day to get the percent of calories from fat.

Finding fat. It's not unusual to find sugar-free cookies and other desserts marketed specifically to people with diabetes. They're sugar free but more than 60% of their calories can come from fat. Here's a good rule of thumb—a food that has less than 5% of the Daily Value of fat or saturated fat is desirably low in fat. (See page 153.) Read labels that say "no cholesterol" or "pure vegetable shortening." These products may still be high in saturated fats. There is saturated fat in all animal products such as butter, egg yolks, whole milk solids, lard, and meat fat. The only vegetable products high in saturated fats are palm oil, palm kernel oil, cocoa butter (chocolate), coconut oil, solid shortening, and partially hydrogenated oils. These fats are found in pancakes, biscuits, cookies, crackers, cake mixes, and some snack chips. Baked goods or frozen yogurts labeled sugar free almost always have calories from fat to make them taste good.

Preferred fats. Unsaturated fats (monounsaturated and polyunsaturated) are thought to be heart healthy (at least compared to saturated fat). They are found mostly in plant foods and are liquid at room temperature, whereas saturated fats are solid. Examples of polyunsaturated fats are corn, cottonseed, sunflower, safflower, and soybean. Olive, canola, and peanut oils are monounsaturated fat and are thought to be the best choices in a healthy diet. Choose a low-fat margarine that has water or vegetable oil as its first ingredient rather than a partially hydrogenated oil. Hydrogenating an oil makes it solid and spreadable but also makes the fat more saturated. Hydrogenated margarine has 0.6 g saturated fat per teaspoon and butter has 2.5 g/tsp.

Vitamins and Minerals

The recommendations on vitamin and mineral supplements for people with diabetes are the same as for the general population. If you're eating a variety of foods, you're likely getting all the vitamins and minerals you need. Large doses of micronutrients have not been shown to help diabetes or blood glucose control unless the body is suffering from a shortage in the diet.

Your Meal Plan

Remember, healthy food choices for you are healthy food choices for everyone else. Your family and friends can all benefit from joining in with your food choices, lower-fat cooking techniques, and meal ideas. Your eating plan is likely to affect your entire family's eating habits, both what and when they eat. Their health almost certainly will improve if they follow your meal plan. One parent with type I diabetes, who had raised her children on three meals and two snacks a day, wondered whether they ever realized that they didn't have to eat that way.

Why visit a dietitian? To develop meals just for you. Even if you're an old hand at planning meals, products change and you change. As you grow older or your lifestyle changes (the kids grow up, you decide to train for a half-marathon, you plan a trip through Europe), your dietary goals will change. Maybe you need a new approach. A dietitian can help you learn any of these approaches to food:

✦Counting calories
✦Counting fat
✦Counting carbohydrates
✦Counting sodium
✦Counting Exchanges
✦Tightening your blood glucose control, and
✦Meeting specific nutritional goals.

A dietitian knowledgeable in diabetes care (perhaps a Certified Diabetes Educator [CDE]) can suggest new ways to look at food. Maybe you want to lose weight and count fat grams. Or, you want to count carbohydrate grams to better match your insulin to the rise in blood glucose that follows. With your dietitian's help, you can determine:

✦About how many calories you should eat each day.
✦About how many carbohydrates you can eat each day and keep your blood glucose levels within range.
✦About how many grams of fat you need to eat to keep your fat intake at less than 30% (only 10% saturated fat) of calories on average.
✦New ideas for breakfast, lunch, dinner, and snacks.
✦How to adjust your meals for exercise.

✦How to handle food changes for sick days.

You may want to try out some meals already measured and counted for you—like those in the Month of Meals series of books (see Resources, pages 250–251). Trying to figure out how to match your food choices to these guidelines looks like a daunting task. Keep in mind that developing a workable meal plan takes time and some trial and error.

Shopping Smarts

When you go grocery shopping, you don't want to waste your time or your money. Food labels are a way to get the nutrition information you need. Once you and your dietitian have set your daily goals for calories, fat, saturated fat, cholesterol, and carbohydrate (and perhaps fiber and sodium), you'll find information about all of these on every food label.

As you shop, you can compare foods by the Nutrition Facts panel. Looking at the label (Table 1), you'll find the serving size, the number of calories per serving, and the calories from fat. Below this information and on the left are the actual number of grams or milligrams of fat, cholesterol, sodium, carbohydrates, and protein in one serving. On the right, you find the % Daily Value. This tells how much of the recommended total daily intake you use up when you eat *one serving* of this food. These numbers are for a 2,000-calorie diet. Your numbers may be slightly higher or lower depending on how many calories you need each day. If you are on a 2,000-calorie diet, a cup of chili gives you:

✦8 grams of fat (3 grams are saturated fat),
✦72 calories from fat, or
✦13% of your recommended fat for the day.
(See Table 1)

Table 1. Chili with Beans

Nutrition Facts

Serving Size 1 cup (253 g)
Servings Per Container 2

Amount Per Serving
Calories 260   Calories from Fat 72

	% Daily Value
Total Fat 8g	13%
Saturated Fat 3g	17%
Cholesterol 130mg	44%
Sodium 1010mg	42%
Total Carbohydrate 22g	7%
Dietary Fiber 9g	36%
Sugars 4g	
Protein 25g	

Vitamin A 35%	Vitamin C 2%
Calcium 6%	Iron 30%

*Percent Daily Values are based on a 2000-calorie diet. Your Daily Values may be higher or lower depending on your calorie needs.

Ingredients: water, beef, beans, tomatoes, modified food starch, chili powder, salt, sugar, flavoring

1 Starch/Bread Exchange, 3 Lean-Meat Exchanges, 1 Vegetable Exchange

Eating the whole can (2 servings) would provide 144 calories from fat or 26% of your daily fat limit. One serving gives you 22 grams of carbohydrate or 7% of the amount of carbohydrate you're trying to eat each day.

Under the heading Total Carbohydrate is 4 grams of sugars. These include both the naturally-present sugar in the tomatoes and the added sucrose. All sugars—whether added or naturally present—are listed in Nutrition Facts. This means the lactose in yogurt and the fructose in fruit juice (naturally-present sugars) show up as sugars on the labels.

Health Claims

Manufacturers can only make health claims on food labels that are supported by scientific research. For example, that

✦calcium may prevent osteoporosis,

✦reducing fat and cholesterol may reduce the risk for coronary artery disease,

✦reducing sodium may prevent or reduce hypertension,

✦dietary fat may be associated with some cancers,

✦fiber found in fruits, vegetables, and grains may play a preventive role in certain cancers and heart disease, and

✦eating more fruits and vegetables may be associated with lower cancer risk.

Other Claims

Here are some of the nutrient claims you'll see and can now believe on food packages.

Calorie free means that this product has less than 5 calories per the reference amount (usually 1 serving).

Low calorie means 40 calories or less per serving.

Light or **lite** means that the food has one-third less calories or 50% less fat than the foods it is being compared with, usually the full-calorie version of the food.

Less and **reduced** both mean that the food is reduced at least 25% in calories compared with the full-calorie version. When these words are used on a label, the actual percentage must be included, for example 50% less salt or fat reduced by 25%.

Cholesterol free means that the food must have less than 2 milligrams (mg) of cholesterol and 2 grams (g) or less of saturated fat per serving.

Low cholesterol means 20 mg or less of cholesterol and 2 g or less of saturated fat per serving.

Low fat means that a food must have 3 g or less of fat per serving. For example, while vegetable oils are cholesterol free, they are 100% fat. A tablespoon of vegetable oil, although preferable to butter or lard because it has less saturated fat, still has about 14 g of fat and the same 126 calories of the butter or lard.

Fat free means that a food has less than 0.5 g of fat per serving.

Low saturated fat means that a food has 1 g or less of saturated fat per serving and not more than 15% of its calories from saturated fat.

Low sodium means 140 mg or less of sodium per serving and per 100 grams of food. Salt is not the only source of sodium; it's found in monosodium glutamate (MSG), sodium bicarbonate, sodium nitrate, and sodium nitrite, and occurs naturally in some foods.

Very low sodium means 35 mg or less of sodium per serving and per 100 grams.

Sodium free or **salt free** items have less than 5 mg of sodium per serving.

Light in salt means the product has 50% less sodium than the regular version.

Sugar free means that you'll get less than 0.5 g of sugars per serving.

Dietetic does not have a standard definition. It means only that something has been changed or replaced. The item may contain less sugar, less sodium, less fat, or less cholesterol than the same regular product. If you look closely at the ingredients list of a package of dietetic cookies, you might find that they are only low in sodium and not low calorie or sugar free, as the name implies.

Natural has no clear definition except on meat and poultry products, where it means that no chemical preservatives, fillers, hormones, or the like have been added. On labels of other foods, the word natural is not restricted in its meaning by government regulatory requirements.

Fresh can apply only to raw food that has not been frozen, heat-processed, or preserved in another manner.

A Healthy Shopping List

Bread. Choose low-fat varieties that list whole grains as the first ingredient on the label.

Cereal. Choose varieties that list whole grains first on the label, and contain

✦4 or more grams (g) of fiber,

✦1 g or less of fat per serving, and

✦5 g or less of sugar per serving.

  TIP: Cooked oatmeal is the cheapest, heathiest choice ever.

Crackers and snack foods. Whole grains first on the label, and

✦2 g or less of fat per serving (5 to 12 crackers).

✦Pretzels or plain popcorn (no cheese, air-popped, 2 g fat or less) are low-fat snacks.

✦Check sodium content per serving.

Rice, pasta, and whole grains.

✦Converted, brown, or wild rice of any type. Most of the vitamins are in the brown outer covering.

✦Unfilled fresh or dried pasta, preferably made with whole-grain flours.

Frozen desserts. 3 g or less of fat per 4 ounce serving (1/2 cup).

✦Low-fat frozen yogurt or low- or nonfat ice milk.

✦Frozen fruit juice bars with fewer than 70 calories per bar.

✦Avoid foods with cream of coconut, coconut milk, or coconut oil (high in saturated fat).

Milk. Skim or 1% milk—lower in fat.

✦Buttermilk made from skim milk.

✦Low-fat and nonfat yogurt, artificially sweetened.

Cheese. Skim-milk and reduced-fat cheeses with 6 g of fat per ounce or less.

✦Try skim-milk mozzarella, low-fat Farmer's cheeses,

✦Nonfat or low-fat ricotta, and

✦Nonfat or 1% fat cottage cheese.

Red meat. Beef, veal, and pork are labeled by animal, body part, and type of cut: for instance, pork loin chops.

Meat is graded based on its fat content: Prime (highest in fat), Choice, or Select (lowest in fat).

Choose lower fat grades of meat, such as **Select**, and **lean** body parts,

✦Beef—round or sirloin

✦Pork—tenderloin

✦Lamb—leg

✦Chicken or turkey—without skin, especially white meat

TIP: Ask your butcher to cut 4 ounce servings of raw meat. In cooking it will shrink to a 3-ounce serving size.

Luncheon meat. Lean or 95% fat-free meats (by weight), with

✦30–35 calories per ounce, and

✦1 g of fat per ounce.

Poultry. Boneless, skinless breast meat is leanest of

all.

Removing skin before cooking cuts fat by 1/2 to 3/4 and cholesterol by 12%.

Turkey or chicken as salami, bologna, hot dogs, and bacon, can be high in fat. Look for 30% fat or less.

TIP: Look for ground turkey that is less than 7 to 8% fat by weight (36% or less of its calories from fat), because often the fatty skin may have been ground in, too.

Seafood. Fresh fish or shellfish.

✦Clear eyes, red gills, shiny skin, and no "fishy" smell.

✦Shrimp is usually shipped frozen to preserve freshness.

✦Canned fish packed in water or with the oil rinsed off. Look for low-sodium products.

Vegetables. Fresh and frozen vegetables are most nutritious per bite.

Drain and rinse canned vegetables to reduce sodium content.

Fruit and fruit juice. Fresh, frozen, or dried fruit.

✦Freshly squeezed 100% pure fruit juice (fresh, canned, bottled, or frozen concentrate).

✦A label saying "made **with** 100% juice" or "juice drink" may list other ingredients. Look for "no sugar added." Check the Nutrition Facts and take the carbohydrate from sugars into account.

Margarine and **oil**. Water and/or vegetable oil first on the label.

✦Olive, canola, soybean, safflower, sesame, sunflower, or corn oils.

✦1 g or less of saturated fat per serving (usually a tablespoon).

✦Light and diet margarines differ between brands in amount of fat per serving.

Salad dressings. Try reduced-calorie and fat-free types.

Sour cream and cream cheese. Try nonfat or light

sour cream. Try nonfat or low-fat yogurt flavored with chives, herbs, or spices.

Soup. Look for low-sodium, reduced-fat varieties.

Cookies, cakes. 3 g or less of fat per 100 calories. TIP: Sometimes fat-free cookies have more calories than the original recipe because of added sugar. Avoid palm, coconut, and hydrogenated oils.

Angel food cake is made without fat and has no cholesterol but does have sugar. Other cakes can be made without cholesterol by using egg substitutes but usually not without fat. Some substitute applesauce or nonfat yogurt for oil.

TIP: Try using nonstick vegetable cooking spray for cooking and cut back on oil. Invest in seasonings and condiments: they add flavor but not calories to your meals. Try the good taste of fresh herbs for flavor.

Dining Out

Eating out is definitely part of our lifestyle today. Restaurants are responding to health-conscious guests by providing food lower in cholesterol, fat, and sodium.

✦If you don't know the ingredients in a dish or the serving size, don't be afraid to ask.

✦Try to eat portions similar to what you would eat at home. Some restaurants allow you to order smaller portions at reduced prices. If larger portions are served, put the excess in a "doggie bag" before you begin or share with your dining companions.

✦Request that no butter or salt be used in preparing your foods.

✦Ask that sauces, gravy, salad dressings, sour cream, and butter be served on the side (or left off altogether).

✦Select broiled, baked, poached, or grilled meats and fish rather than fried. If food is breaded, peel off the outer coating, where the extra fat is.

✦You can request substitutions, such as low-fat cottage cheese, baked potato, or even a double portion of a vegetable instead of french fries.

✦Ask for low-calorie items, like low-calorie salad dressings or broiled, steamed, or poached fish instead of fried, even if they're not listed on the menu.

✦Adjust insulin dose for changes in your meal plan.

Problem Solving

If you are:

✦**Eating later than usual.** If you cannot change the timing of your insulin dose, eat a piece of fruit or a starchy, low-fat snack from that meal at your usual mealtime. Always carry snacks with you—don't leave home without them. If you plan to go out for brunch, eat an early-morning snack, and then use your lunch meal plan and what's left of breakfast at brunch. If dinner is to be very late, have your bedtime snack at your normal dinner time. You will need to adjust your short-acting insulin doses to do this.

✦**Eating more often than usual.** At holidays, when it feels like you're around food all day long, and in social situations which may increase your tension levels, divide your total food for the day into snack-size meals. Then you can spread the food out a little more than usual while nibbling throughout the day.

✦**Eating more food than usual.** Parties or visiting friends may tempt you to overeat. Overeating or eating sugary or high-fat party foods can make you feel guilty. But you don't need to feel guilty. Even if you never go off a strict diet, you're going to have swings in your blood glucose levels. At times like these, remember you've got other blood glucose managment tools. Use them. Plan more physical activity before or after the event. Consider taking more short-acting insulin to cover the extra calories.

Eating While Traveling

How do you adjust to unpredictable occurrences while traveling, like a train breakdown or a delay in meal service on a plane?

✦Don't take mealtime insulin unless you are sure you can follow it with food.

✦Carry a snack pack with crackers and/or cheese, granola bars, peanut butter, fruit, and some form of sugar (hard candy) or glucose tablets. This emergency snack will be handy in case of low blood glucose.

✦If you plan to change time zones, talk with your health-care team about timing your meals and insulin injections.

✦For some people who want to vary the times they eat on a daily basis, intensive insulin therapy may be the answer. See Chapter 4.

✦Pre-order a special (low-fat) meal when making your plane reservations.

Eating Disorders

Eating disorders are more common among people with diabetes than the general population. Why? The physical and emotional demands of controlling your food constantly or always having it controlled for you can lay the foundation for food abuse. Actually, people with diabetes do tend to weigh a bit (about 10 pounds) more than their peers, especially those whose diabetes is tightly controlled.

Eating disorders occur most often among young people whose sense of worth comes only from having a perfect weight and shape. The normal weight gain at puberty, at diagnosis, or with tight control, the time many eating disorders start, makes some people with diabetes resort to extreme measures to stay thin.

There are two main eating disorders, anorexia nervosa and bulimia, each with its own set of warning signs. A person with anorexia refuses to eat in order to stay thin. People with bulimia will eat, often excessive amounts, and then purge the food from their bodies through vomiting or laxatives. Both disorders weaken and stress the body and deny it the nutrients it needs.

People with eating disorders have more episodes of ketoacidosis and hypoglycemia, and their glycated hemoglobin levels tend to be higher. The risk of nerve damage, neuropathy, is therefore higher, too. If you have an eating disorder, get medical help by talking to your doctor or mental health professional, and look for a local support group to help you.

Alcohol

There is little evidence that an occasional mealtime drink is harmful to people with diabetes in good control. But, having even one alcoholic drink on an empty stomach can lead to a low blood glucose reaction.

Alcohol affects both the way insulin acts and the way the liver produces glucose. The liver converts stored carbohydrates and then protein to glucose when blood glucose levels decline. The liver also clears toxins such as alcohol from the body. The body gives priority to this clearing role, delaying glucose release for a time and putting you at risk for a low blood glucose reaction unless you have food.

If you drink later in the evening, you will need a large snack before bedtime and breakfast as usual the morning after. It's smart to check your glucose levels before, during, and after drinking. Drinking can result in low blood glucose hours afterwards. For instance, if you eat too little while you are drinking, you may have a reaction during the night or the next morning.

Reasons to Avoid Alcohol

Some people with type I diabetes have a problem storing glucose in the liver or releasing it from the liver. So, they already have less defense against low blood glucose reactions, which alcohol can aggravate. Alcohol can make other medical problems worse and should be avoided if you have:

✦Neuropathy. Alcohol is directly toxic to nerves. If you have peripheral nerve damage in your arms or legs, heavy or regular drinking can increase pain, numbness, and other symptoms. There is some evidence that even regular light drinking (less than two drinks per week) is harmful.

✦Gastric problems. Alcohol can increase the discomfort of chronic bowel problems due to autonomic neuropathy such as diabetic diarrhea or constipation.

✦Hypertension. Alcohol makes your blood pressure increase because it causes vessels to constrict. If you already have hypertension, cutting out even light alcohol consumption may reduce your blood pressure.

✦Retinopathy. Heavy drinking (three or more drinks a day) is associated with the development and progression of eye disease.

✦High triglycerides. Alcohol affects the clearance of fat from the blood by the liver and encourages the liver to produce more triglycerides. Even moderate amounts of alcohol (two 4-oz. glasses of wine a week) can raise triglyceride levels in the blood.

✦Other complications. These include liver disease, pancreatitis, some heart or kidney diseases, and problems with pregnancy.

Drinking is not recommended before exercise because alcohol constricts the vessels of the heart, limiting the amount of oxygen available to exercising muscles. Be sure to eat if you combine exercise with social gatherings that include alcohol. Both alcohol and exercise can push blood glucose too low.

Be aware that alcohol also affects motivation. You may find that even one glass of wine with dinner makes you less interesed in accomplishing anything else that evening from folding the laundry to monitoring your blood glucose levels.

Nine

Fitness Fits in With Diabetes Care

Exercise is the fun part of diabetes management. Any way you do it—walk, jump, jog, ride, skate, bike, climb, ski, or chase the ball—you defend yourself against heart disease and lower blood glucose levels at the same time. Plus, when you're fit, you feel better, you look better, and your body works better. Being fit means you're ready to do anything.

You don't have to run a marathon to be fit. As many ways as people play, that's how many ways there are to gain fitness. Play daily and you're on your way. All you need is an exercise plan based on your health and needs.

Tell Me Again, Why Exercise?

Most important is this: regular exercise strengthens your heart and circulatory system and protects you against the increased risk of cardiovascular disease due to diabetes. Active movement gets your heart pumping and improves the flow of blood through your small blood vessels. People who exercise are less likely to have a heart attack. Exercise helps decrease blood cholesterol levels and increase "good" high-density lipoprotein (HDL) levels. An added benefit is that exercise removes glucose from your blood, both while you are exercising and for several hours afterward. This means that you'll probably be able to use less insulin (or eat more) on days you exercise.

As with everyone, exercise improves physical health and mental attitude. It helps you lose weight and body fat. It's important in preserving bone strength and preventing osteoporosis in women. It's a great stress reliever. It's fun! Exercise is not a cure-all, but it's close.

Before You Start Something New...

Check with your health-care team. To help gain benefits from exercise without drawbacks, it's wise to get the advice of your health-care team when you start or change an exercise program. You may need a physical exam. Almost certainly you will need advice on adjusting food and insulin from a dietitian.

Although almost everyone with diabetes can and should exercise, some activities may be better for you than others. If you have eye disease, kidney disease, nerve damage, or blood vessel disease, you may need to avoid certain kinds of exercises. If you are over 35 or have heart disease, you will need an electrocardiogram, which looks at heart function, before your doctor gives the go-ahead. Your doctor may even ask you to take an exercise stress test to look at how your heart and blood pressure react to a workout. For this test, your doctor may want to refer you to an exercise physiologist.

Exercise physiologists conduct treadmill tests or bicycle testing while checking your blood pressure and heart function; figuring out your percent of body fat; and testing your strength, flexibility, and endurance. Based on this information, they develop exercise programs to fit your schedule and special needs.

Consult with your health-care team to find your answers to these questions:

✦How often shall I exercise?

✦How long shall my exercise session be?

✦How hard shall I exercise?

✦How and when should I monitor how hard I exercise? Should I count my heart rate? Do I know how? What heart rate should I aim for?

✦Are there any types of exercise I should avoid?

✦Are there any symptoms (for hypoglycemia or heart disease) I should watch out for?

✦Are there special precautions I should take?

✦Do I take less insulin or change my injection site before I exercise?

Your Main Concern—Changes in Blood Glucose

Your muscles use glucose for energy. When you first start exercising, your body uses stored glucose in the muscles and liver for fuel. As this runs low, your body looks to blood glucose for fuel. So, during exercise, blood glucose levels can fall. Then after you stop exercising, your body restores glucose to the muscles and liver, further lowering blood glucose levels.

Don't forget that the body can absorb insulin differently from day to day. This means that the same amount of insulin can have effects that differ from any day to the next. And exercise is known to increase blood flow, which can also increase how fast the insulin you inject gets to work.

Because exercise lowers blood glucose levels and can speed insulin in its work lowering blood glucose levels, it's a good idea to test your blood glucose level when you exercise. Otherwise, you can have a low blood glucose reaction without expecting it.

Here are some specific guidelines that will help keep blood glucose in line with exercise:

✦The best time to exercise is 1 to 3 hours after a

meal, when your blood glucose is slightly elevated. Exercising after meals may keep you from needing to eat snacks to exercise.

✦If your blood glucose level is less than 100 mg/dl before exercise, have a high-carbohydrate pre-exercise snack (15 grams of carbohydrate) and test again 15 to 30 minutes later. For example, fruit, juice, half of a peanut butter sandwich, two crackers with thin slice of cheese, or cereal would fit the bill.

✦If your blood glucose level is 100 to 250 mg/dl, exercise. Until you learn the effects of exercise on your body, self-monitor your blood glucose during and after exercise to see whether you need a snack.

✦If your blood glucose is over 250 mg/dl, test your urine for ketones. If ketones are high, this means you do not have enough insulin. You'll need another injection. Do not exercise until ketone levels return to negative or trace amounts. A high blood glucose level can go even higher because of exercise. Hard exercise with inadequate insulin makes the liver release stored carbohydrate, which is turned into glucose for fuel, despite high blood glucose levels.

✦You may want to know which way your blood glucose level is heading, especially if you're about to start an activity where you can't easily "pull over," such as scuba diving, sailing, or skiing. Test 1 hour, then 30 minutes before you start. If your tests tell you that your blood glucose level has come down, even if the latest test says it's in the safe range, you may want a snack to keep it from going any lower. Know when your insulin is peaking.

✦Eat an extra amount of carbohydrate (10–15 grams) after 30 minutes of exercise if you plan to continue exercising and if the exercise requires endurance, such as running, aerobics, squash, or racquetball. Have a snack for every additional hour that you exercise. If the exercise is very intense and long, such as a marathon, you may need to eat 10 to 15 grams of carbohydrate every 30 minutes. Good snack choices are foods high in carbohydrate and low in fat, such as fig bars, yogurt, or soups rather than sugary sweets. Fresh fruit, which has a high water content, is also a good choice.

✦If you feel a low blood glucose reaction coming on while exercising, **stop exercising**. Take some form of fast-acting sugar. Do not make the mistake of thinking you can last a little while longer. Some fruit juice or a regular (nondiet) soft drink will provide sugar as well as replace water lost during exercise.

✦Always carry some glucose gels or tablets, raisins, or hard candy just in case you need it when exercising.

✦Know the action time of your specific insulin(s). Take into account the types of insulin you use and the timing of injections, exercise, and meals. Try not to exercise when your insulin is working its hardest unless you've eaten.

✦Remember, hypoglycemia can happen not only while you are exercising but up to 24 hours after you stop working out. Monitor your blood glucose levels to prevent yourself from having a low blood glucose reaction.

Adapting to Your Own Needs

The more you exercise, the more your body adapts. Check your blood glucose to see whether you really need extra carbohydrates before exercising. If you exercise regularly, try to make the snack a part of your usual meal plan. It is not always desirable to eat a lot of extra food as snacks, especially if you're try-ing to lose weight.

Some athletes reduce their insulin dose before exercising instead of eating extra food. This works especially well if you exercise for an hour or more at a time. Speak to your health-care team about cutting your insulin dose for the exercise you have planned.

If your blood glucose level is highest in the morning, try exercising after breakfast. If you like to exercise before dinner, see whether you need an afternoon snack before you exercise. If you are an evening exerciser, you may decide to reduce your insulin before dinner, have a larger dinner, or plan a snack during exercise or at bedtime.

Safe, Effective Exercising

Listen to your body. You should not have too much fatigue, pain, or shortness of breath during your workout. Doing too much too fast can lead to injuries that may keep you from doing anything at all. Follow commonsense guidelines (Table 1).

Typically, a workout session should have 5 to 10 minutes of warm-up exercises and stretching, followed by 20 to 30 minutes of aerobic exercise, and finally 5 to 10 minutes of cool-down exercises and stretching. Daily stretching will increase your flexibility. Aerobic exercise--in which you keep your body moving--benefits your heart, lungs, and muscles. It is the best way to use up calories for a weight-loss program. To see improvement, work out at least 3 times a week.

Exercise burns calories. Also, exercise increases your body's basic rate of metabolism not only while exercising but for several hours afterward. That's why exercise is an important part of any weight-loss plan. However, exercising too hard or cutting way back on the calories you eat to lose weight are not advised for anyone and are especially dangerous for you. If weight loss is one of your personal goals, a sensible reduction in calories and a regular exercise program will have the best results.

Warm-up phase. Get moving slowly, with low-intensity movements. Once your muscles are warm, gentle

Table 1. Safety Guidelines for Exercise

❖Know your blood glucose levels.

❖Try to exercise with a friend or, when you exercise alone, at least let people know when you are going out, where you will be, and when you will be back.

❖Warm-up and cool-down each time you work out.

❖Remember to replace body fluids. Water is the best fluid replacer.

❖Carry visible diabetes identification and money for a phone call.

❖Use well-fitting footwear, and check your feet every day and after each exercise session.

stretching without bouncing is recommended. Don't stretch when your muscles are cold because you may injure them. For example, in a walking program, walk at a normal pace for about 5 to 10 minutes, then stop and do some stretching. Gradually increase the intensity of the workout until you reach the aerobic phase.

Aerobic phase. During an aerobic workout, your muscles require more oxygen. The heart has to beat faster, and you work your cardiovascular system to pump oxygen and blood through your body's small blood vessels. During this phase, your heart rate should be kept higher than normal for about 20 to 30 minutes. Aerobic activities are continuous, such as walking, jogging, swimming, and bicycling. Activities where you get to stop and start, such as bowling, golf, weight lifting (usually), and baseball, do not qualify as aerobic activities because they do not keep the heart rate elevated.

Cool-down phase. The cool-down gradually slows

your heart rate and breathing as your movement slows. Stretch out your muscles again while they are warm.

Pacing Yourself

One way to find the pace that is best for you is to know and work out at your target heart rate. This is the heart rate per minute that is best for aerobically conditioning your heart and lungs. A simple calculation below gives you a way to determine this target zone based on your age.

1. Measure your heart rate while at rest by counting the number of beats your heart makes in 1 full minute first thing in the morning before you get out of bed. This is your resting heart rate (HR_{rest}).

2. Find your maximum heart rate by subtracting your age in years from 220 (220 - age = HR_{max}).

3. Put these numbers into the formula: HR_{max} - HR_{rest} = $HR_{max\ reserve}$. This gives you your maximum heart rate reserve.

4. Multiply HR_{max} reserve by 0.5 and 0.7 to determine 50% and 70% of your heart rate reserve. When added to your HR_{rest}, this gives you the lower and upper limits of your heart rate during an aerobic workout. For example, a 40-year-old (220-40 = 180 = HR_{max}) with a resting heart rate of 75 would have a heart rate target range of 128 to 149. (See below.)

	Lower Limit	Upper Limit
HR_{max}	180	180
-HR_{rest}	-75	-75
$HR_{max\ reserve}$	105	105
x intensity	x 0.5	x 0.7
%$HR_{reserve}$	53	74
+HR_{rest}	+75	+75
Target HR	128	149

In this example, this person would look for a heart rate between 128 and 149 beats per minute to be working at 50 to 70% of aerobic capacity.

An important note is that this calculation does not take into account any of your specific health conditions or medications that affect your heart rate.

For instance, if you have problems with the nerves that control your heart rate, or take a medication that alters your heart rate, you can't get your target heart rate by this method. Your doctor or exercise physiologist should advise you on the target zone that is right for your condition. This may require you to have exercise stress testing.

Walking. Walking is the best, safest, and least expensive form of exercise for most people. It's exercise that can fit into anyone's schedule. In exchange for a good pair of walking shoes and attention to foot care, you get an exercise that conditions the cardiovascular system, the lungs, and the muscles of the arms, legs, abdomen, lower back, and buttocks. Walking is a life-long activity, and it is a good way to ease back into a more active lifestyle. After walking for awhile, you may have the confidence, stamina, and fitness level to try other activities.

Start walking for 10 to 15 minutes and gradually increase your time. Don't set mileage goals. Work on lengthening the time you spend walking, and eventually, your mileage will increase. At the start, it may take you 30 minutes or so to walk a mile. An expert walker can walk a mile in 8 to 12 minutes. A pace of 4 miles per hour or 15 minutes per mile is a good goal to work toward.

Jogging. Some people would rather jog than walk. But jogging is tougher on your joints and feet because each step pounds the foot with three to five times your body's weight. Before jogging, take the time to develop your leg and foot muscles. Avoid jogging on concrete; try the local high school track instead. Buy a pair of well-padded running shoes and replace them before they are worn out. These precautions will help you prevent injury.

Strength training. You can reverse or help prevent flabbiness by reducing your body fat and toning your muscles. Weight training is one way to build and keep up muscle strength. Use a weight that is heavy enough so you tire after lifting it eight or nine times. Move up to a heavier weight if you can lift one 15 times with ease. Don't hold your breath as you lift. It's best to get instruction from a weight-lifting expert. You don't have to lift heavy weights to get a benefit. Many repetitions with a small weight will tone your muscles, too. Be aware that some complications may be made worse by lifting heavy weights. That's why you check with your health-care team first.

Foot Care

Check your feet daily for any red, irritated areas, blisters, corns, calluses, or ingrown toenails. Take care of problems right away. Well-fitted shoes will help keep problems from starting. Buy shoes designed for the activity you choose. Shoes should feel comfortable right away. Don't count on "breaking them in." If you have decreased sensation or neuropathy in your feet, you can't trust the way shoes feel as you try them on. You may need to consult with a podiatrist to get a correct fit.

Don't forget about socks. There are special socks designed with extra cushioning for exercise, but any good athletic sock that is made of a blend of cotton and synthetic material will provide warmth and cushioning and will absorb perspiration away from your skin. Start each workout in a clean pair of socks.

Ten

Family Planning and Pregnancy

Planning a pregnancy is essential. You increase your chances for a successful pregnancy dramatically when your blood glucose levels are as normal as possible from the first moments of pregnancy to delivery. This also gives you the best chances of having a healthy baby. This is why your pregnancy needs to be planned.

Birth Control for Women

Your options for birth control are about the same as anyone's. Which form of contraception you use is up to you and your partner. The pill, diaphragm plus spermicidal jelly, sponge, and condom plus spermicidal foam are all good ways to prevent pregnancy. Sterilization is the choice for people who want to prevent pregnancy from ever occurring, because it is nearly impossible to reverse. Your doctor and gynecologist should be able to help you decide which method is best for you.

The pill. Oral contraception, or the birth control pill, is one of the most popular methods of birth control. However, popularity doesn't mean the pill is best for you. The advantage of birth control pills is their reliability. They are 98% effective when taken as directed.

Birth control pills contain a combination of estrogen and progesterone, two female hormones that are important for the menstrual cycle. This combination pill is the oral agent of choice for women with diabetes if the estrogen dose is less than 35 micrograms. If you take the hormones for 21 days out of the usual 28-day menstrual cycle, the release of the egg (ovulation) will be prevented.

The pill was introduced in the early 1960s, and there has been some controversy over its short-term and long-term side effects. Some of the suspected side effects are an increased risk for heart problems, stroke, and blockage of the blood vessels in the lower legs. For these reasons, the pill has been studied since it became available more than 20 years ago. Researchers have found that for most women, the risk of taking the pill is far less than the risk of an unwanted pregnancy or a pregnancy that occurs at the wrong time. However, for women with diabetes, the pill is still suspected of increasing the risk of complications. A low estrogen dose can minimize these risks.

However, if you are over 30 and smoke, or you have a history of heart disease, stroke, hypertension, or peripheral vessel disease (such as phlebitis), the pill presents still more risks and may not be for you.

Norplant System. This is a series of capsules containing the hormone progesterone that are inserted under the skin. They can remain in place releasing the hormone for up to 5 years with no maintenance. This system is about 96 to 99% effective in preventing pregnancy. The downside is that the treatment is very expensive and it causes menstrual irregularities in about 25% of the women who use it. Ask your doctor whether this method would be a good choice for you.

IUD. The IUD, or intrauterine device, is a small plastic device that is placed just inside the opening of the uterus by a physician. Because IUDs have been linked with infections, doctors generally do not recommend IUDs for women who have diabetes. However, the newer T-shaped copper-containing IUD may be appropriate for older women with diabetes who have finished childbearing. You should discuss with your doctor the benefits or risks involved in using an IUD. When properly inserted, IUDs are about 97% effective.

Diaphragm. The diaphragm is a small rubber cup lubricated with a spermicidal gel and inserted into the vagina before intercourse. It fits over the cervix and acts as a barrier to prevent sperm from entering the cervix and passing to the uterus and possibly fertilizing an egg. For this reason, the diaphragm is called a barrier method of birth control. After intercourse, the diaphragm should stay inside the woman's body for 6 hours. Because the diaphragm can be placed incorrectly, it's only about 82% effective in preventing pregnancy. Be sure you are trained to place it properly and can check that it is covering the cervix.

Sponge and cervical cap. The sponge, also a barrier method, is small and contains sperm-killing gel. It is placed in the vagina before intercourse. It is only about 72% effective. The barrier methods (IUD, diaphragm, sponge) work only when they are correctly in place. Different methods can be used together to increase effectiveness.

The cervical cap is smaller than a diaphragm but also fits over the cervix preventing sperm from entering the uterus. When placed properly, it has about 82% effectiveness in preventing pregnancy. However, it may be related to abnormal Pap smear results.

Female condom. A larger type of condom, another barrier method, has been developed for women. It is inserted into the vagina before intercourse and is removed afterwards, taking the sperm with it. It can protect against sexually transmitted diseases.

Rhythm method. The least dependable method of birth control, the rhythm method, requires the most effort. In general, it works when a woman avoids intercourse for 3 to 4 days around the time she ovulates. Unfortunately, it takes a great deal of training to know when ovulation occurs, and the woman must be closely in tune with her normal monthly menstrual cycle. Your gynecologist can teach you about this birth control method. For every 100 women using this method, 20 to 30 become pregnant.

Sterilization. In a procedure called tubal ligation, doctors surgically tie off the fallopian tubes and prevent eggs from reaching a woman's uterus. This is nearly 100% effective in preventing pregnancy. In very rare cases, a fertilized egg may reach the uterus, resulting in pregnancy. Or it may begin to grow outside the uterus, requiring surgery. This birth control option is chosen by people who do not want to have any more children, because it is very difficult to reverse.

Birth Control for Men

Men have birth control options available to them as well. You can wear a condom, a thin piece of rubber that fits over the penis before sex and keeps the sperm from entering the woman. The condom, when used with spermicidal foam, is about 88% effective in preventing pregnancy if used correctly each time you have intercourse. The condom should be removed soon after sex. Condoms can also protect against sexually transmitted diseases.

If you believe he does not want to father any more children, he can choose to have a vasectomy. A vasectomy is a simple operation that prevents sperm from leaving the man's body, and therefore, prevents pregnancy. It is very difficult to reverse a vasectomy, so most men do not choose this option until they and their children are older.

Glucose Control and Menstruation

The menstrual cycle affects some women's insulin needs. Most commonly, women find they have unusually high blood glucose levels in the few days before flow begins. Treatment requires extra insulin during those days. On the other hand, you may be used to having low blood glucose reactions during this same time. In either case, it's a good idea to examine changes in your eating habits related to your menstrual cycle, like desiring fatty or salty foods or loss of appetite.

Unusually high or low blood glucose levels can also be caused by temporary changes in insulin sensitivity at different times in the menstrual cycle. Some women find relief from this with oral contraceptives that give out a fixed dose of hormones throughout the month. This is especially helpful for women with irregular cycles.

Will My Child Have Diabetes?

No one knows why type I diabetes occurs. There is evidence that having a parent with diabetes slightly increases a child's risk of having diabetes. This risk is different depending on whether the parent with diabetes is the father or the mother.

The baby of a mother with diabetes who is 25 years old or older has a 1% risk of developing diabetes. This is not very different from anyone's chances of developing type I diabetes. If the mother is younger than 25 years old at the time the child is born, the risk increases slightly, to about 4%. If the father has diabetes, the child's risk of developing type I diabetes increases to about 6%. Each of these risks is doubled if the parent developed diabetes before age

11. If both parents have type I diabetes, the risk is not known, but is probably somewhat higher.

Pregnancy

The key to a successful pregnancy is excellent diabetes control both before and during pregnancy. When your blood glucose is in the normal ranges, even after meals, the baby has the best chance of being healthy (see Table 1). The baby's organs are formed during the first 6 to 8 weeks after conception. It is critical to have normal blood glucose levels at this time to prevent birth defects. After this time, good glucose control prevents extra glucose from making the baby grow too large. Healthy babies from diabetic mothers are a lot more common than they used to be. This is because more women with diabetes and their doctors are working to normalize blood glucose levels before and during pregnancy.

This extra effort starts before pregnancy. For best results, your pregnancy must be planned. Birth defects occur in 6 to 12% of the infants of women with diabetes as compared to 2 to 3% of babies of nondiabetic women. In addition, women with diabetes are more likely to have stillbirths and infants with other health problems. These risks can be greatly lowered (although not completely removed) with normal blood glucose levels and good care both before you

---

Table 1. Blood Glucose Goals for Pregnancy Complicated by Diabetes

Fasting	60–90 mg/dl
Premeal	60–105 mg/dl
1 h after meals	110–130 mg/dl
2 h after meals	90–120 mg/dl
0200–0600	60–120 mg/dl

From *Medical Management of Pregnancy Complicated by Diabetes*, Alexandria, VA, American Diabetes Association, 1993.

conceive and during your pregnancy and delivery.

Your Medical Team

The ideal health-care team for your pregnancy includes your doctor, an obstetrician interested in the treatment of pregnancies complicated by diabetes, a pediatrician interested in the care of infants of mothers with diabetes, and a dietitian. To find names of such health-care providers, talk to your doctor or other mothers with diabetes or contact your local chapter of the American Diabetes Association.

Prepregnancy Exam

You need to get a thorough physical exam by your doctor before you become pregnant. Your doctor will be looking for any health problems that could endanger your health or your baby's. This includes high blood pressure, heart disease, kidney disease, and eye disease. All of these problems should be treated before you become pregnant. Pregnancy can sometimes make them worse. Or they can lead to other problems, such as stroke or heart attack. In addition, your doctor should take a blood sample to measure your thyroid function and to measure your glycated hemoglobin level, which shows your overall glucose control.

If you've had diabetes for more than 10 years and you have symptoms of heart disease, such as chest pain, your doctor may want you to have an electrocardiogram. Your doctor should also look for signs of damage to nerves (neuropathy) that control things like heart rate and blood vessel opening and narrowing. This diabetes complication can affect how your heart and blood pressure will react to the physical stress of pregnancy. Because neuropathy can also affect how well your body supplies nourishment to you and your growing baby, tell your doctor if you have nausea, vomiting, or diarrhea.

Your prepregnancy exam should include your kidneys. In some women, kidney disease may get worse during pregnancy. If you have impaired kidney function, you should know pregnancy may be more difficult for you to manage and you may be troubled by edema (swelling) and high blood pressure.

An ophthalmologist should examine your retinas (the part of your eye that collects images) through dilated pupils to look for damage due to diabetes (retinopathy). Eye disease should be treated before you become pregnant. Diabetic retinopathy may develop or get worse during pregnancy, but can be treated during pregnancy, so continue to have eye exams during pregnancy. Retinopathy tends to return to its prepregnancy status after delivery.

All this medical care is expensive. But, the cost of a pregnancy complicated by diabetes is much less than it used to be. Before self-monitoring of blood glucose, a woman spent half of her pregnancy in the hospital, and the bill was about $40,000. Now the major expenses are for fetal monitoring and blood glucose testing instead of hospitalization and loss of salary.

Self-Care

It's important to fine tune your blood glucose levels. After-meal blood glucose levels become more important. You'll probably test eight times each day: once before each meal, 1 or 2 hours after each meal, at bedtime, and around 2:00 a.m. Meal planning will take on a high priority.

You may need to change the kind of insulin you take and how often you inject it. Usually, the amount of insulin you need increases with each trimester. This is normal and does not mean that your diabetes control is getting worse. Most likely, you will return to your previous insulin routine as your body recovers from the pregnancy.

It's worth it to pay a special visit in the planning stages to your dietitian to get help making dietary changes to meet the demands of pregnancy. Your tighter diabetes control plan will affect how you eat. You may need to switch to three meals and three snacks a day. Or, you may need a middle-of-the-night snack. A weight gain of 22 to 32 pounds over the 9-month period is normal. If you are very overweight, your doctor may advise you to limit your weight gain.

Pregnant women can usually exercise by walking, swimming, and doing other low-impact aerobic exercises. You'll probably be able to keep doing any exercise you were doing regularly before pregnancy, but your physician should approve any exercise you want to do. Toward the end of your pregnancy, you can ask your obstetrician to show you how to check whether the exercise you do causes you to have contractions of your womb. These contractions mean you're overdoing it.

If you have morning sickness there are some dietary steps you can take to help yourself feel better (see Table 2). Usually, nausea is worse when the stomach is empty–which is ususally morning. For this reason, keep some starch, such as melba toast, rice cakes, saltines, or other low-fat crackers on your bedside table so you can eat if you become nauseated in the night or early morning. Eating a protein and

Table 2. Tips for Controlling Nausea

✦Eat dry crackers or toast before rising
✦Eat small meals every 2.5–3 hours
✦Avoid caffeine
✦Avoid fatty and spicy foods
✦Drink fluids between meals, not with meals
✦Take prenatal vitamins after dinner or at bedtime
✦Always carry food

From *Medical Managment of Pregnancy Complicated by Diabetes*, Alexandria, VA, American Diabetes Association, 1993.

carbohydrate snack at bedtime, such as cheese and crackers or half of a sandwich, will help prevent early morning nausea. To keep your stomach full, you and your health-care team may decide six small meals a day would work better for you. Generally, each meal should include food sources of carbohydrate, protein, and fat.

The Birth

At one time, babies of women with diabetes were delivered before or during week 37, because waiting raised the child's risk of death or delivery problems. This was due to the large size of the babies born to mothers with high blood glucose levels during pregnancy. Now that self-monitoring and tight blood glucose control are the rule during pregnancy and there are special tests to monitor the baby more closely, infants are more likely to remain in the mother's womb until labor and delivery occur naturally.

Sometimes, even with tight blood glucose control, the baby is too large or the mother's pelvis is too small for her to deliver vaginally, and a cesarean section (C-section) is performed. A C-section is an operation in which a cut is made through the lower abdomen and uterus to remove the baby. Good glucose control during pregnancy can help keep the baby from becoming too fat and decrease your chances of a C-section. If you have a C-section, you will need to stay in the hospital 4 to 5 days. It often takes 6 weeks to fully recover, because a C-section is major surgery.

Most women don't need insulin during active labor. After delivery, your blood glucose levels should be checked regularly to find out when you should start taking insulin again.

After Delivery

The most important part of your postdelivery regimen is follow-up care with your diabetes doctor. Although some new mothers actually have better control in the first 6 to 12 weeks after delivery, for many moms it's a period of unpredictable blood glucose swings. These swings are usually caused by normal postdelivery changes in your hormone levels. Try not to get discouraged and let the good blood glucose control habits that you developed during your pregnancy slip away. Your baby needs a healthy mother!

Remember that you can become pregnant again soon after you give birth. Even if you have not had a menstrual period, you still may ovulate. Many people believe that breastfeeding your baby will prevent you from becoming pregnant. This is not always true. Before you are ready to resume intercourse, you also need to resume birth control.

Many parts of your life are altered with the baby's arrival, but the four basic diabetes management tools remain the same: insulin, blood glucose monitoring, meal planning, and exercise.

Exercise may get less of your attention at this time. Fatigue, erratic schedules, and limited mobility or discomfort—especially after a cesarean delivery—make it difficult for you to use exercise to control your blood glucose levels. But as soon as you feel well enough, a daily walk will make you feel better.

Highs and Lows

You may want to stay with your pregnancy blood glucose testing schedule. Hormonal changes, emotional shifts, irregular sleep patterns, and fatigue may mask or change symptoms of high or low blood glucose. Clues that once told you that your blood glucose level was high or low may no longer appear.

Clearly, when you have a baby in your care, it's

wise to test for low blood glucose and treat it right away. Keep sugared items such as hard candy, regular soda, or glucose tablets handy in several rooms, especially where you usually sit down to nurse. Make sure that anyone helping you knows the symptoms of low blood glucose and what to do if you don't seem to be yourself.

You may have difficulty telling the difference between "after-baby" emotional reactions, such as moodiness or unexplained crying, and low or high blood glucose. Fatigue, feeling spacey, weakness, or forgetfulness can be caused both by high or low blood glucose, and by physical and emotional changes. When you're not sure, play it safe and test.

If you have a history of being unable to detect low blood glucose levels, be particularly careful not to let your blood glucose get low when you are alone with your baby. Remember, your best protection is still regular snacks and meals, appropriate insulin doses, and frequent blood glucose monitoring. Don't nap or go to sleep with an empty stomach.

You may find that your baby's erratic schedule and your own chaotic sleep patterns make it difficult for you to eat or snack at the times you need to. You can be so busy following your infant's eating pattern that you don't realize when you ate last. But good food and timing of meals is crucial to your diabetes control. Don't put your infant's feeding time before your own dietary needs. Concern for your own health is good for you and your baby.

Breastfeeding

Breast milk is the ideal nourishment for a new baby. (And breastfed babies have a lower incidence of type I diabetes.) Your diabetes should not stop you from successfully breastfeeding your baby, but breastfeeding may complicate your glucose control. Your body uses a lot of energy to make breastmilk. This could cause your blood glucose levels to be more erratic. Or, you may find the opposite is true, that diabetes is easier to control and you can eat more and take less insulin. Be aware that your symptoms of low blood glucose can be different while you are breastfeeding and can appear without any warning.

Therefore, you'll need to test your blood glucose level often in the months that you breastfeed. You should also take extra precautions to have a fast-acting sugar (carbohydrate) handy if you notice low blood glucose symptoms while you're breastfeeding.

When your baby is ready to be fed during the day, eat your own snack—or meal, if it is your meal-time—as you feed your infant. It helps to have the snack or meal portion ready so you don't have to prepare anything while the baby is waiting to be fed. Snacking or eating this way provides your body with fluids and helps prevent low blood glucose.

During one of the baby's night feedings, again, have a snack yourself. Otherwise, you might find you have low blood glucose the next morning, especially if you feed the baby several times during the night.

Eleven

Your Working Life

Y ou are teachers, cooks, athletes, nurses, man-
agers, electricians, even truck drivers. The list
of jobs for people with type I diabetes is almost
endless. It wasn't always so. If you had been looking
for a job in 1930, you would have been turned down
for any position with the federal government. In fact,
until 1989, just having a parent with diabetes kept
you out of military service. Only in the 1990s have
such blanket bans become rare. With the passage of
the Americans With Disabilities Act, which concerns
your right to private employment, and the Federal
Rehabilitation Act, which concerns your right to federal government employment, more and more doors
are opening for people with diabetes. Go after any job
you feel qualified for.

Your Schedule

Are you in the office from 9 to 5, or do you work by
the light of the moon? Diabetes doesn't have to
decide your schedule. As long as you monitor your
glucose level, irregular working hours and night
shifts should be manageable. It's true that your diabetes-care plan will be simpler if you have a regular
routine. But you can pair a more unpredictable
lifestyle with diabetes. You will have to spend more

money and time on blood testing and making adjust-ments, but you do not have to be restricted in your work schedule options. So, feel good about yourself, and stress to your employers that your take-charge approach toward diabetes also means you will be an even better employee.

The Night Shift

Night shifts do pose a challenge for people taking insulin. If you have to work them, you will need to change your insulin regimen to fit your work and food schedule. Imagine you're a nurse working the 11 p.m. to 7 a.m. shift at a hospital. Obviously, if you come home at 8 o'clock in the morning with plans to sleep through the day, you will have to change your morning insulin dose, because you won't be eating lunch at noon. Taking the normal dose would put you in danger of hypoglycemia while you sleep. Your health-care team can help you make changes, such as adding longer-acting insulin to your morning dose and reducing or eliminating short-acting insulin (depending on your eating schedule). If your job requires some nights on and some nights off, then you will need to test your blood glucose more often and possibly use multiple injections or an insulin pump. Blood glucose monitoring will let you fine-tune your therapy to allow for an erratic schedule.

Dangerous Equipment

It's important to test your blood glucose often before and during work if you operate dangerous equipment or drive. An insulin reaction in these situations can cause severe injury, to yourself and others.

The federal government still does not allow people who take insulin to enter the armed forces, to pilot airplanes, or to drive trucks or buses on interstate highways. Each of these policies is under review, however, and people with good records of blood glucose control may soon be able to accept these types of jobs.

Some guidelines on driving:

✦Check your blood glucose level before you leave your house. If it's low (70 mg/dl or less), treat it. Retest 15 minutes after your first test to be sure your blood glucose is rising and that you are safe to drive. If not, treat again and wait till your blood glucose is normal. Take along a snack in case the level drops later on.

✦Always carry some fast-acting source of carbohydrate with you—raisins, glucose gel or tablets, or hard candy. If you feel even minor symptoms of low blood glucose while driving, pull over and do a blood test. Being a few minutes late is better than being in an accident.

✦If you're unable to check your blood glucose and you feel hypoglycemic, do not drive until you treat it and the symptoms pass. It's a mistake to think you can hold out until you get wherever you're going.

Long-Distance Travel

If your job requires travel, there are a few things you should know. If you are traveling by airplane and have some advance warning, you can order special low-sugar, low-salt, low-fat, or low-cholesterol meals. Airlines want to meet your needs, but they need at least 48 hours notice.

On the plane, don't inject your premeal insulin until you see the meal cart coming down the aisle. A bumpy flight or air traffic can delay your meal. Bring snacks with you in case your meal gets delayed.

Air travel can be dehydrating, so it's a good idea to drink lots of water. Remember that drinking alcohol will only add to the dehydration.

Flying across time zones may be a little confusing. In general, when you lose hours from your day (traveling east from California to New York), you may need to reduce or skip a dose of insulin. When adding hours to your day (traveling west from New York to California), you will probably need an extra dose of insulin. Ask your doctor to supply sample routines to try.

Your health-care team can help you adjust your intermediate- or long-acting and short-acting insulins for travel days. What you decide to do will depend on your meal schedule and plans for sleep or activity when you get to your destination. Self-monitoring of blood glucose while traveling is the best way to deal with uncertainty.

Advance Planning Is the Key

✦If you travel often, you may want to carry a letter from your doctor (on letterhead paper) saying that you have diabetes. Be sure the letter includes a statement that you must use insulin and syringes and blood glucose monitoring supplies.

✦A prescription from your doctor for insulin may come in handy if you start running low while you're out of town.

✦You can always look up your local ADA affiliate or chapter in the white pages of the phone book if you're traveling in the United States. If you're going overseas, write for a list of International Diabetes Federation groups.

✦Wear a medical ID bracelet or necklace that says that you have diabetes.

✦If you're leaving the country, learn how to say "I have diabetes" and "Sugar or orange juice, please," in several languages so you can make yourself understood wherever you are.

✦If you need medical attention and have a choice,

you may want to contact the nearest American consulate, American Express, or local medical school for a list of English-speaking doctors.

✦To be safe, pack twice as much insulin and blood-testing equipment as you think you'll need. Pack half in your carry-on luggage to keep your medications with you.

✦If you find yourself running low on insulin while abroad, remember that insulins sold outside the United States are often lower than the U-100 used in the United States. If you buy insulin that is a different strength (U-40 or U-80), you must buy new syringes to match the new insulin to avoid dosing errors. If you use U-100 syringes for U-40 or U-80 insulin, you will be taking too little insulin. Conversely, if you use U-100 insulin in a U-40 or U-80 syringe, you will be taking too much.

✦Don't get separated from your medical supplies. Get used to carrying a tote bag, fanny pack, or backpack with your insulin, syringes, meter and lancets, glucose gel or tablets, and some food.

Discrimination

Unfortunately, discrimination against people with diabetes still exists. Throughout your career, employers may hesitate to hire you. However, the Federal Rehabilitation Act and the Americans With Disabilities Act require employers to give an equal chance to people with disabilities.

Under these laws, diabetes is legally considered a disability or a handicap. It's tough to think of diabetes as a disability, but in this case, the definition helps defend your rights. The law defines a disabled person as one who

✦has a physical or mental impairment that substantially limits one or more major life activities,

✦has a record of such an impairment, or
✦is regarded as having such impairment.

If you work for a private employer who has 15 or more employees and you feel you have been discriminated against because of diabetes, the Americans With Disabilities Act gives you the right to file a complaint with the Equal Employment Opportunity Commission (see Resources, page 264) and have the situation corrected.

In the past, applicants often had to list their specific medical conditions on a job application. The employer could then refuse to hire based on this medical information. The applicant would not know if the decision was based on a bad recommendation, not meeting qualifications—or diabetes.

Now, an employer can ask an applicant medical questions and require medical exams only **after** making a job offer, and only if this is done across the board for all applicants. Then an employer may withdraw a job offer only if the applicant, for medical reasons, cannot perform the essential functions of the job even if reasonable accommodations are made by the employer.

The law requires employers to try to accommodate people with disabilities. For instance, employers may need to build ramps or elevators to provide access for people who use wheelchairs. For people with diabetes, employers may have to adjust work schedules or establish breaks for blood glucose testing so that employees can manage their diabetes on the job.

Once you've started work, an employer can ask only medical questions that are job-related and consistent with the needs of the business. For instance, if an employee falls asleep on the job, an employer may ask if a medical condition is the cause. However, if an employee doesn't look well but is performing his or her job, an employer may not ask whether there is a medical problem.

Fighting Back Against Discrimination

People who believe they have been discriminated against in their jobs may file charges with the Equal Employment Opportunity Commission (EEOC). The EEOC has free information booklets for the public and employers (see Resources, page 264). Other organizations have produced resources about the Americans with Disabilities Act or have set up information lines. You may wish to contact them (see Resources, page 265).

Other sources for potential help in dealing with claims of job discrimination are listed in Table 1.

If you believe you have been discriminated against in your job, whether in hiring, firing, promotion, tenure, or other aspects, you can file complaints with the United States Attorney General. The attorney general files lawsuits on behalf of citizens to stop discrimination. An employer may have to award you money, reverse the discriminatory decision, and pay penalties. If you choose to bring a private lawsuit against the company afterwards, money can't be awarded.

A successful job discrimination claim has to be based on fact. It is up to you to prove that you have been discriminated against because of diabetes. The best evidence is a written statement from the employer or person who made the decision. Write to request a written statement saying why you weren't hired or promoted or were let go. There may be other reasons for the employer's decision, and your attorney will need to know about them. You will very likely need an attorney's help with this claim.

Gather together materials such as the employer's job application form, policy manuals, or statements regarding the employer's position on equal employment opportunity and any rules or regulations cited by the employer as the reason you were dismissed or not hired. Save copies of the job advertisement or listing, the job description, and the job performance evaluation criteria.

You should also make a list of potential witnesses, including their work titles and how to reach them. Include some information about their duties at work and how they would know about your situation. Finally, make a diary of the events in chronological order as they happen.

Table 1. Sources to Contact in Case of Discrimination

✦Your state's Human Rights Commission or Equal Employment Opportunity Commission: most states have a commission charged with investigating discrimination.

✦Your union representative: if your job requires union membership, your union may have an Employment Discrimination Office.

✦Your state or local Department of Labor or Employment: there may be someone responsible for investigating job discrimination claims.

✦Your state or local bar association: they may be able to help you find an attorney who handles job discrimination cases pro bono (at no cost to the client) or offers other legal assistance.

✦Your state American Diabetes Association Affiliate: some affiliates have created a network of attorneys who will represent or help find counsel for people with diabetes who are being discriminated against in finding or keeping a job.

To Tell or Not to Tell

Whether you tell your employer about your diabetes is completely up to you. Some people do not understand diabetes and may make things difficult for you. On the plus side, being open about your diabetes can teach others and reduce the false notion that people with diabetes are less capable than others. Also, because you take insulin, your coworkers should be able to tell when you have low blood glucose and how to treat it.

If your work schedule needs to change, your employer may be more sympathetic if he or she knows you have diabetes. By being open earlier, you may show your employer that you are a responsible employee. Always explain that as long as you control your blood glucose levels, you will be able to do your job.

The Job Hunt

Don't let fear of discrimination in the workplace prevent you from seeking out or reaching your career goals. When seeking a new job:

✦Don't regard your diabetes as a defect. But also don't hesitate to assert your special needs in the workplace.

✦Prepare ahead of time by knowing your rights. For instance, remember that employers may not ask questions about your health before deciding whether to hire you. Once they've offered you the job, however, they can ask health-related questions as part of the employment physical examination.

✦If you wait to disclose your diabetes until you've been offered a job (this is your legal right), take a positive approach. Refer to any awards you received in previous jobs or point out how few sick days you've ever taken. If you exercise regularly to stay fit, you may want to describe your routine.

✦When you disclose your diabetes during your physical exam (if you're required to take one), present a truthful picture of your condition and your control. Don't change your treatment plan immediately before the examination. Changes in routine can affect control of your diabetes. Remember that the company's doctor is probably not a specialist in diabetes care. Point out the steps you take to maintain control of your diabetes.

If your diabetes forces you to change careers, and you are unable to afford retraining, you can get training through State Departments of Vocational Rehabilitation. Your local American Diabetes Association Affiliate will help you find the programs that are available in your state.

Hopefully, popular thinking will catch up with what we already know about people with type I diabetes: that with good blood glucose control, people can do anything they're qualified for, from scuba diving to performing surgery.

Twelve

Insuring Your Health Care

Health care in the United States is so expensive that health insurance is a must for all Americans. For you, diabetes can make medical care extra expensive, even if you have insurance. Finding the best possible coverage is important not only to your pocketbook but to your health. You'll want to find a plan that meets your needs and your budget.

However, because you need help with both routine and unexpected costs, you are expensive to insure. The health insurance situation for people with type I diabetes can be discouraging. At this writing, the government is working on a national health-care plan that would make it much easier for people with diabetes and other medical problems to get and keep health insurance. But under the current system in the United States, if you are new to a job or to retirement, you will discover that new health insurers focus on diabetes and label it a "preexisting condition." They may exclude your diabetes from coverage for an extended period of time—from 6 months up to 3 years—or they may charge you higher premiums than people who do not have diabetes, or they may refuse to cover you at all. For this reason, it is not wise for you to leave your old insurance—and perhaps the employer who is supplying it to you—until you have secured a new job and health insurance.

What's Your Policy?

You can gain health insurance in many ways. Ideally, your employer covers all or at least most of the cost of your insurance. But for different reasons, many people are not covered through an employer. It is critical to think about health insurance whenever you change jobs, move, or make another big change in your life. Don't get caught without insurance, even briefly. Insurance in case of illness is like having an umbrella in case of rain. The day you don't bring your umbrella, it will rain.

You may obtain insurance through an employer, or you may purchase transition coverage known as COBRA, a conversion policy, a stop-gap policy, individual coverage, or pooled-risk insurance. The possibilities are discussed below.

Through Employment

You may have the option of joining a group policy offered by your employer. Group policies are usually open to all employees, regardless of their health. The Americans with Disabilities Act requires that if an employer grants insurance to one employee, it must make the same policy available to all employees. Coverage by employers with fewer than 15 employees may require health screening and medical history. Your employer may pay most or all of the insurance premium for you. For an additional fee, these policies may also cover your spouse and children. Health care is considered a nontaxable expense, so if you pay a fee for health-care coverage, you may have it taken from your paycheck before taxes are taken.

The Transition Period

Maybe you need insurance to cover you while you make the transition from school to work, or from job to job, or from work to retirement. A federal law called the Consolidated Omnibus Budget Reconciliation Act (COBRA) may help you. COBRA demands that your employer allow you to keep your insurance policy with equal coverage for up to 18 months after you leave your job. You will have to pay for the coverage and may be charged up to 2% more than the rate the company was charging your employer. But this is almost always less expensive than purchasing a new short-term policy. If you are disabled, COBRA coverage can be extended to 29 months. This legislation applies not only to employees but also to dependents, who can continue their coverage for up to 36 months. Recent high school or college graduates who have not yet secured insurance of their own may be able to take advantage of this law to provide coverage while searching for a new job and during the exclusion period for preexisting conditions.

You have 60 days after you've been laid off or have left the company to accept COBRA benefits. During that 60 days, employers are obliged to keep paying insurance bills incurred by employees and their dependents. Employers with fewer than 20 employees, the federal government, and churches are exempt from COBRA. If you are ineligible for COBRA, or if your COBRA coverage runs out, you have some other options.

Many states require employers to offer you a conversion policy regardless of your physical condition. (Fifteen states and the District of Columbia do not require this action.) In most states if an insurance company terminates a company's group plan, it is required to offer you a conversion policy as well.

When you convert your policy, you remain with the same insurer but begin paying for your own insurance. Conversion coverage is almost always more expensive than your group plan and provides fewer benefits, but it may be your only choice for coverage. You have 31 days to accept or reject this coverage after the COBRA runs out or you leave your job. For that reason, you need to explore your insurance options as much in advance as you can.

You can also purchase temporary short-term health-care coverage on your own. A stop-gap policy generally lasts for 1 year and is designed for people between jobs. Shop around with various insurance companies to get the best price for the most coverage.

On Your Own

There's no way around it: your diabetes makes health insurance a necessity. If you are not eligible for any form of group insurance, finding an affordable individual policy can be difficult. Individual policies are contracts between individuals and an insurance company. Insurers do take your medical history into consideration when they decide whether to enroll you. Some states allow health insurance companies to offer bare-bones policies to small businesses and individuals. These policies cost 30 to 40% less than major-medical policies and provide fewer benefits, but they may be of help to you. You may also be able to find insurance through a professional or trade association of which you are a member. For instance, the Student Nurses Association provides health insurance to nursing students and any dependents at a less expensive rate than either colleges or private companies.

Another Resort

Have you been turned down for insurance? Certain

states offer "pooled-risk" health insurance for people who have lived in the state for 6 to 12 months and have been rejected for group or individual coverage. The coverage is good, but the costs of pooled-risk insurance varies widely among the states that offer it. Most try to keep it affordable by placing limits on the premium. The cost will still probably be higher than individual coverage. Some states have waiting lists to buy into the pool. See Resources, pages 267–270, for a list of states with insurance risk pools.

Traditionally, Blue Cross and Blue Shield Companies have been considered the insurers of last resort—meaning they will insure anyone, regardless of health problems—especially for people in states without pooled-risk insurance. But only one-fourth of these companies now hold open enrollment periods when anyone may apply for coverage, and many exclude preexisting conditions from coverage for a year or more, just as other insurance companies do.

Insurance and Diabetes

Your insurance policy is a contract, and you should read it carefully to see what it provides. It allows partial coverage (with co-payment) for doctor's visits, annual or semiannual physical exams, durable medical equipment, prescription drugs, and medical supplies. But read the policy to be sure.

If your health insurance covers durable medical equipment, it should pay for a blood glucose meter, a fingerstick device, an insulin injector or syringes, and an insulin pump if prescribed by your physician as "medically necessary," unless the policy specifically excludes these items. Your physician will have to give you a thorough explanation in writing of why each of these items is necessary for you. This is your "prescription" for these items.

If your insurance covers prescription medications and/or medical supplies, it usually will pay for insulin, lancets, glucose meter strips, and insulin pump supplies, if you have a prescription for them. Whenever you have to purchase medical supplies or equipment, it is a good idea to ask the company in advance. Be sure to record the name of the person who answers your questions along with the date, in case you should need this information to appeal a denied claim.

You, Your Policy, and Your Doctor

However you are insured, there are different agreements between insurance companies and doctors. Some agreements limit your choice of doctor in exchange for a better-priced plan. The major types of plans are fee-for-service and managed care.

Traditionally, health insurance companies ask you or your employer to pay a set amount of money (premium) each year and let you decide what doctors and hospitals to choose. In these **fee-for-service** plans, the insurance company will pay for some or all of your medical care. But the company will not usually start paying for your care until you have paid a small amount for it out-of-pocket, a deductible. You are also usually responsible for a portion of the cost of a visit or services (the copayment). Most plans reimburse at 100% after an out-of-pocket expense limit is met.

The advantage of the fee-for-service approach is freedom to choose among a wide range of health-care professionals and area hospitals with whom your insurance company is affiliated. The disadvantage is that preventive health care, for example a mammogram or Pap smear, is usually not covered.

In **managed-care** situations, your insurer—in an attempt to hold down costs—will carefully examine and approve what kind of tests and procedures you need to have done and when you need to see a specialist. Your primary-care doctor will often make these recommendations. Managed-care plans are usually **prepaid**, meaning that you and/or your employer pay a fixed premium and you receive comprehensive health care, from routine office visits to hospitalization. Your cost is lowest if you seek care from the network of participating physicians and hospitals. You generally have no deductible to satisfy or paperwork to do. You also will not be expected to pay out large sums of money for services, so you have better control over your budget should unexpected illness occur. Your choice of hospitals is limited if you need anything other than emergency hospitalization. If you wish to see a health-care professional or have a test that is not approved, you may have to pay much of your bill and have your benefits reduced.

Health maintenance organizations (HMOs) are the best-known type of managed-care health plan. HMOs usually create a full-service health center by hiring or contracting with health-care professionals to work in their buildings. You must usually see someone under contract to or employed by the HMO to receive prepaid health care. The HMO makes arrangements for coverage for sickness or accidents when you travel outside the HMO's service area.

A **preferred provider organization (PPO)** is another kind of managed-care plan. A group of doctors agree with an insurer (often a Blue Cross and Blue Shield plan) to discount their fees. They are then paid by the insurer and by a small fee, usually $5 or $10, that you pay when you visit. You may choose your doctor from among those who have joined the PPO, and you are seen in that doctor's private office. If you want to use a doctor outside of this network, you may have to pay most of the bill and may lose benefits in the future as well.

Medicare and You

If you are over 65, disabled so that you cannot work, or have a very low income, you may have other insurance options. The federal insurance program, **Medicare**, covers a portion of hospital bills, doctor fees, and other expenses for people over age 65 and some people who cannot work because of disabilities. If you get Medicare, you will still have to pay for a large portion of your bills.

You can sign up for Medicare 3 months before the month of your 65th birthday. Contact your local Social Security Administration office, listed under the United States Government listing in your telephone book. Bring your birth certificate when you apply.

Not everyone over age 65 can get Medicare. For example, some people who worked at state or local government jobs are not eligible for Medicare. Check with your local Social Security Administration office if you are unsure about coverage.

If you have a very low income, you might be eligible for **Medicaid**, a federal and state assistance program. Medicaid regulations vary from state to state, so you'll have to contact your state's Medicaid office to find out whether you qualify and what health expenses will be covered. A social worker can help you with this.

How Medicare Helps With Hospital Bills

Once you are enrolled in Medicare, the plan can help pay part of your hospital bill. Under Medicare Part A, you must pay a deductible—about the average cost of a 1-day stay in a hospital. In 1994, the deductible was

$696; this was up from $676 in 1993. You pay the deductible for each spell of illness that requires hospitalization; if you have been out of the hospital for 60 days, your next visit would be considered a new spell of illness.

After that, Medicare pays the full cost of your first 60 days in the hospital. It pays for a semiprivate room and the cost of such things as nursing services, medical supplies, lab work, X rays, and medicines.

If you are still in the hospital after 60 days, Medicare keeps helping. But you must start paying part of the bill. If you are in the hospital for more than 90 days, you must start paying the entire bill. You do have lifetime reserve coverage to keep Medicare helping with the bill after the 90th day, for 60 more days. But once those extra 60 days are "spent," they cannot be renewed.

Medicare will not pay for long-term nursing home care. Medicare Part A can help pay for short-term "skilled nursing care." Many nursing homes do not provide what Medicare defines as "skilled nursing care." So Medicare will not approve or pay for most nursing homes. To find out whether a nursing home is approved by Medicare, check with your local Social Security Administration office or the nursing home itself. Medicare will pay for hospice care for those who are terminally ill.

How Medicare Helps With Doctors' Bills

Medicare Part B can help pay for a portion of your doctors' bills. You make a monthly contribution (about $41 per month in 1994). People who receive Social Security have this amount withheld from their monthly Social Security checks. There is also a yearly deductible of $100, which you must pay before Medicare benefits begin.

After the deductible is satisfied, Medicare will pay

80% of the approved cost. You must pay the remaining 20%. Ask your doctor whether he or she accepts the assignment of a Medicare claim. If they do, you will only need to pay out your 20% copayment, and the doctor will accept the rest of the payment directly from Medicare based on Medicare's estimate of the prevailing charge for that service. If your doctor does not take assignment of a Medicare claim, you can be charged up to 120% of the prevailing charge (but that's the legal limit). You also may have to pay the entire bill yourself and wait for Medicare to reimburse you for 80%. This usually takes six to eight weeks.

How Medicare Helps With Diabetes-Care Expenses

Under Part B, Medicare pays for some diabetes supplies.

✦Medicare will pay 80% of the cost of blood glucose meters for people prescribed insulin, as well as for lancets, strips, and other supplies used with the meter. It will pay for test strips only if you are using a meter. You must have a written prescription for all of these items—over the counter or not—from your doctor, as well as a written statement from your doctor detailing your diagnosis, fluctuations in your blood glucose levels, and your recommended self-monitoring schedule. Make copies of these written statements; you must give a copy of it to your pharmacist for your Medicare claim to be submitted each time you purchase these supplies.

✦Medicare will pay for diabetes outpatient education in some states if particular criteria are met, such as if the program is in a hospital, if the education is considered medically necessary (for example, the primary care physician should write a "prescription" for education), and if the facility and program provider

are Medicare approved.
✦Medicare will pay for foot care.
✦Medicare will pay for laser treatment for diabetic retinopathy (eye disease) and for cataract surgery.
✦Medicare will not pay for insulin or syringes.
✦Medicare will not pay for insulin pumps.
✦Medicare will not pay for outpatient nutrition counseling services or dietitian services in most states.
✦Medicare will not pay for regular eye exams or for eyeglasses.

How Medigap Plans Help

To fill the gaps in your coverage, you can choose from many so-called Medigap plans that pick up some or most of the charges Medicare won't cover. Medigap plans are private health insurance. There are federal standards that insurance policies must meet in order to be called a Medicare supplement policy. Be sure to read the policy carefully and comparison shop before buying one of these plans.

The booklet *Guide to Health Insurance for People With Medicare*, written by the National Association of Insurance Commissioners and the Health Care Financing Administration of the Department of Health and Human Services, is updated every year and is available through any insurance company. Ask for it. It contains the federal standards for Medigap policies and general information about Medicare. A more detailed explanation of Medicare is available as *The Medicare Handbook* from any Social Security Administration office (see Resources, page 265, if you prefer to write away for it).

Dealing With Denied Claims

Even when you think you know exactly what is

and what is not covered by your health insurance, you may still be surprised by a claim returned to you marked DENIED. A fair resolution is more likely if you have the paperwork to support your claim.

First of all, check to be sure that you and your physician have filled the claim form out correctly. If there's nothing wrong with the form, then get your paperwork in order. Be sure you have a prescription from your doctor for every piece of equipment you need—even if it does not require a prescription at the drugstore. Sometimes, submitting the prescription and a copy of your receipt will support your claim enough to get it paid. Then, some companies will want a letter of explanation from your doctor. Never send the original documents to your insurance company. Send them copies of all pertinent paperwork by registered mail so you know that they have been received.

You will have received an explanation of benefits form if all or part of your claim is denied. This form gives the company's reason for the denial and states that you have 60 days in which to appeal this decision. Your next step will be to write to the claims manager of your insurance company by name explaining what is wrong. State for which items they have denied payment, and ask for a written response to your request. Give your address and your phone number as well as your physician's. Send your physician a copy of your appeal request for his records. State that you will call the insurance company on a certain date if you have not received a reply by then. On that date, if you have to, call the claims manager and discuss your case. A wait of two to three weeks would be reasonable.

Perhaps a clerk denied your claim because he or she was using out-of-date information that does not include the newest equipment for diabetes care. Requesting an appeal moves the decision from a clerk to people who should have more familiarity with the newest blood meters, test strips, and other equipment. If you are denied again, don't give up! Request an insurance hearing.

Your state insurance department has a consumer-complaint department and can apply pressure on the insurance company to respond to your request. If you work for a company that does not use a health insurance company but is self-insured (many large companies, unions, and local government workers are), you should appeal directly to your personnel manager or head of the company first. Often they can easily remedy the situation, but if the claim is still denied, write to the state labor department.

Most state insurance commissions have an individual who handles complaints and will provide you an opportunity for a hearing. (See Resources, page 266 for a list). This is where your paperwork is most important. Write to the state commission listing

✦the name of your insurance company,

✦the coverage provided in your policy as you understand it along with a copy of your policy,

✦a description of what happened—send copies of all letters or details of phone conversations between you and the insurance company, and

✦a specific request for a hearing to determine the insurance company's responsibility for payment.

An insurance hearing is like a court hearing in that both you and the insurance company state your case and you must submit copies of all the documents you sent to the commission. Some people represent themselves; some have lawyers. A decision may be reached right away or in the following weeks. If you are not satisfied with the outcome, you may take your case to small claims court.

Every small claims court system has a different way of handling these cases, so you must ask about the procedure. The number will be listed in the city or county government section of the telephone book. The judges there understand that most people represent themselves and will need to hear your side of the story and see copies of your documents. If you want the help of a lawyer, contact your state's American Diabetes Association affiliate. They may be able to help you locate one.

Two organizations can advise you about your situation: the National Insurance Consumer Helpline, operated by insurance industry associations, and the National Insurance Consumer Organization, which is a nonprofit, non-partisan organization (see Resources, page 266).

Thirteen

Reflections on Life With Type I Diabetes

These first-person stories of life with type I diabetes orginally appeared in *Diabetes Forecast*, the members' magazine of the American Diabetes Association.

Why Me?

It was awful.

I hated being there, lying in a hospital bed at the age of 27. I could hardly recognize myself in the mirror, weighing in at a mere 72 pounds. And I had trouble comprehending the horrifying words I heard coming out of the mouth of my doctor: "You have diabetes, Ramona."

Everything he said after that point might as well have been spoken to the wall. My then husband-to-be, Richard, was sitting next to my bed, my parents alongside. Could they translate the doctor's message for me? What was going on?

Just a short three months before I had weighed 40 pounds more, and was recovering from respiratory problems and injuries from an auto accident. But this was something else again. My hands shook so badly, I couldn't hold onto a cup. I was experiencing incredible thirst and nausea, which my physician at first thought could have been caused by my pain medication. And now this, those doctor's words: "You have diabetes." I thought to myself, I don't want to live like this. Why me?

Over the next few days I was taught how to give myself injections and how to test my blood glucose levels. Slowly but surely, my appetite came back, and so did my weight.

But there were little things that had changed about me; things I hated. My vision had become blurry and I couldn't read labels on boxes or drive myself to the store. I was told that it would take some time for these conditions to improve because of my high glucose levels, and I felt angry and impatient. Whenever I was alone, I would cry about my new way of life and the struggle I faced adjusting to the daily routine.

Richard called several times a day, not always knowing what to expect as I swung between bouts of triumph and tears. He bought me a pair of extremely strong dime-store magnifying glasses, so I could see well enough to fill my syringes and read a label. Together, we attended diabetes classes at the hospital and gathered all the information we could to better understand this disease. In time, my glucose levels improved, and in turn, so did my vision. Slowly, the pieces of our lives came back together.

Many months later, as I sat across the table from Richard while he carefully drew the insulin for my dinner injection, I realized I was not alone in my anguish. Across from me sat my nurse, my supporter, my emotional bodyguard, my confidant, my one-man support group. As I watched him doing this task that had become second nature, I felt overwhelmed. Here was the one person who knew my triumphs and my pain.

There had been long days for him, when I had been too ill or too weak to comb my hair or to dress myself. There were times my rage erupted like a volcano as I dealt with hopelessness and despair, knowing I would never be the same person I was before. There were also long nights when my blood sugars would drop rapidly. Richard instinctively woke when he thought my breathing seemed irregular or my body felt clammy. There were nights when he rushed to the refrigerator for juice and helped me hold the glass when I shook so badly I couldn't hold it myself. He took countless trips with me to the doctors and specialists. He encouraged me to take charge and to speak up when I felt a treatment wasn't meeting my needs.

I had become so accustomed to his faithful support that I never realized how difficult it would have been for me if he hadn't been there by my side. I had never once considered the impact my diabetes had on him. On some days, he carried the burden of this illness when I felt I could not. He never hinted that he was unsure of our lives together or that we couldn't handle the obstacles this disease created.

It's now been three years since that day at the dinner table. I no longer think of diabetes as a burden, but as a way of life. And as with anything in our lives, some times are good and others are trying.

I think we all draw strength from somewhere deep inside where we've saved it up until that very moment when we need it most. This strength is grounded in love and faith. These are found in the simplest acts: a few words of support or kindness, or that careful filling of a syringe by someone who wants to assure you that you don't have to go it alone. As I sit across that same table and look at the man who has given so much, sacrificed so much, and nurtured so much, I once again ask Why me? But this time, my grateful heart requires no response.

-Ramona Goldman

The Wall

When I was diagnosed with type I diabetes at age 18, I became suddenly, keenly aware of having joined the ranks of the "handicapped," the "limited," the "flawed." Driving home from the doctor's office, my mother advised me to keep "our secret," for my condition would cost me friends, suitors, and jobs. At our Thanksgiving family gathering, my aunts and uncles spoke in hushed tones of my "condition" and thanked God for the remaining "whole" offspring in the clan.

Insulin dependent, "impaired," I no longer belonged to the Whole World. There was a wall dividing the Perfect People and the Compromised People. My Medic Alert necklace flashed my disability: DIABETIC. I could not eat, play, work, or even sleep without consideration of my limitation. My body didn't work properly. I was defective.

The wall between me and the Perfect People seemed so obvious, so solid, so sturdy. I was struggling along with others who were "abnormal" and dependent to succeed in the world of the healthy and independent.

Of course, I was always happy to see a "fellow flawed" succeeding in the Whole World. One morning I was half-watching a news program while putting on make-up. I paused, mascara wand in hand, and gave my full attention to a legless man who was competing in a marathon. The TV camera focused on the man's powerful arms directing his wheelchair across the finish line. "Good job," I thought, grinning. "You gave the Perfect People a run for their money!"

Mascara wand still suspended, I watched the newscaster interview one of the winning runners. The tall athlete turned his head aside, sneezed, and said, "My allergies nearly got me—the pollen is out early this year!" His face was puffy: he struggled for breath.

The newscaster shifted his microphone to another finisher's face. "I ran this one for my Pop," beamed the athlete. "He couldn't be here today cuz he's in the hospital recovering from a cancer operation."

The newscaster held the microphone up to a third winner. "How's it feel to win?" he asked.

The runner grinned, "Good, man, good! And I wanna say something to Dickie—that's my kid brother. I wanna say 'Dickie, there's more than one way to win!' You see," he confided, "Dickie isn't used to his big brother's winning. I'm dyslexic, can't read. But I can run!"

The camera panned the sunlit crowd. There was a very obese woman standing next to a man with hearing aids. A hyperactive little boy twisted himself around a restraining rail. A woman with bottle-glass spectacles peered into the sun. For a moment, I thought I recognized an old classmate—a girl who had been diagnosed as manic depressive in college. The man beside her looked like my coworker—a chain smoker who couldn't quit even after his wife died of emphysema.

The camera drew back and reduced the newscaster and the crowd to a generic microcosm of humanity. Then, during the commercial break, a parade of laxatives, antacids, and pain killers danced across the screen.

"Good grief, where are the Perfect People?" I thought.

Who do I know who isn't struggling against migraine headaches, arthritis, addictions, or personality afflictions? Was the single mother with shattered self-esteem or the victim of eating disorders any more whole than I?

Suddenly I couldn't find any Perfect People to put on the other side of the wall. I couldn't find any Uncompromised People. After years of thinking diabetes separated me from a privileged class of people without problems, I felt myself merging into a vast array of variously limited, variously challenged human beings.

The wall was gone. I realized that wholeness is not a gift divinely bestowed upon a lucky few; it is, rather, something achieved by those who choose to face life's challenges head on.

We earn wholeness when we see life's obstacles not as walls, but as hurdles. With each hurdle that we jump, we come that much closer to fully realizing our true potential.

-Lurette Kerr

The Lecture

As I backed out of my driveway, I felt like a rebellious teenager being forced to do something against my will. I tried to come up with a good excuse not to keep my doctor's appointment, but my responsible adult self won. "Just get it over with," I thought, "You know what they're going to tell you." As I walked into the office, the smiling receptionist took my name and reached for my blood glucose monitor to make a computer printout. I did a tug of war with her in my mind, trying to decide if it was any of her business. The nurse weighed me, took my blood pressure, then stuck my finger for the inevitable glucose reading. "My, we're a little high today," she said frowning.

I moved to the examining room and listened to the discussions going on around me. Across the hall, there was an elderly man with a patch on his eye. He was holding the hand of his plump wife, their eyes riveted toward the door, listening for the doctor's footsteps. A baby was wailing in the next room, comforted by a mother with another two-year-old attached to her leg.

An intern came in to do my workup, and I remembered I wasn't in the mood for this. He sat down and began asking me questions. "Any headaches, stomach aches, muscle aches, history of heart disease, undue stress?"

I laughed and said, "Just check yes on everything. I'm sure it will happen sooner or later." He glanced at me then quickly continued. I answered with snappy replies, taking pleasure in making him nervous.

After he left, I sat resigned to my coming lecture and examined the computer printout from my meter. "It looks like you're a little high quite often, not just today," I said out loud, mimicking the nurse. But I could feel my rebellion giving way to the old familiar feeling of guilt for not taking control.

I know how to keep my blood sugar in control, but through the years I've found ways to rationalize a certain lack of control. When my children were young, I was afraid of having a hypoglycemic reaction. In a grocery store one day, I had to set my screaming baby in the cart while shocked onlookers watched me drink a can of orange juice right off the shelf. It was an experience I did not want to repeat, and I was willing to let my blood sugar go up a little to avoid it.

Even when my children were older, I still had to deal with a busy schedule, and I didn't want it interrupted by blood tests and shots. I didn't want to be in church or at a meeting that ran longer than expected and have to open a packet of crackers and munch on them while everyone stared.

I often wondered how many people with diabetes actually got a normal A1C blood test. I felt certain that those who did led lives that were completely controlled and inhibited by their disease.

I sat with my head in my hands and tried to come up with more reasons to justify my poor control. There weren't many left. The years of excuses were being replaced by the reality of changes in my vision and some unusual aches and pains.

I listened again to the young mother across the hall laughing with her children, and I knew she also had to juggle them, her home, and her control. I watched the older couple talking softly, worried about his complications and wishing for another chance. Who was I kidding? I had been rationalizing for years and soon it would be too late to turn back the clock. It was taking more energy now to fight the guilt than to fight the disease.

I was still deep in thought when the doctor came in. "Okay, dear," she said, "We're going to have to get tough on you."

"I know," I said, "I've got to keep to my diet plan, cut down on fats, and make sure I exercise three to four times a week."

"Very good," she said. "But most of all, I want you to get rid of the stress in your life. Learn how to take it easy on yourself."

Take it easy? This was not the lecture I had expected. My anger slipped away. As we talked, I began to realize that to really get rid of my stress, to "take it easy on myself," I had to give up those old companions, fear and guilt. Fear had bred the excuses that kept me from dealing with my diabetes, and the guilt that always followed became an overwhelming burden.

Nothing earth-shattering happened to me that day in the doctor's office, but I left with a renewed sense of purpose. For years, I had convinced myself that controlling my diabetes would be a burden. Yet by avoiding that responsibility, I was forced to bear a weighty load of guilt and self-doubt. Keeping my blood sugar in control will be a tough fight, but in the long run, I'm better off fighting diabetes than fighting myself.

-JoAnn Westwood

Almonds and Raisins

When I was a child, and the ups and downs of life overwhelmed me, my mother used to try to comfort me with an old Jewish saying: Life is a mixture of almonds and raisins—the bitter and the sweet. It didn't mean much to me at the time, but now that I am a mother of three and have developed diabetes, I understand what she meant.

From the time of conception, through pregnancy and childbirth, and then on to the struggles of childhood and adolescence, parenting is truly a concoction of almonds and raisins. Parents of children with chronic illnesses and disabilities know the taste of almonds and raisins, particularly the almonds.

But what about parents who themselves suffer from chronic illnesses such as diabetes, especially mothers, who still tend to be the primary caregivers in our society? As a mother with diabetes, I have tasted many almonds and raisins while trying to balance my obligations as a caregiver with my responsibilities for my own health.

Since I developed diabetes almost three years ago, another of my mother's sayings has taken on a new meaning: A mother always saves that last piece of bread for her children. I know that a mother is supposed to be selfless, but a mother with diabetes must also be selfish. I have had to learn, and so has my family, that there must always be a last piece of bread for me. There are some things even a mother can't share, like the juice boxes and granola bars I keep stashed in my purse, coat pockets, and glove box in the car.

When I was diagnosed with type I diabetes, I was advised about exercise and hypoglycemia. I was told that housecleaning, walking, bicycling, and other forms of exercise made it necessary for me to either eat more food or take less insulin. No one ever mentioned boisterous play with my children, a trip to the playground, or even sleepless nights spent nursing a sick child. After I experienced hypoglycemia in situations that I never would have considered as "extra activities," any outing alone with my children began to assume terrifying proportions.

At the time of my diagnosis, my children were 11/2, 5, and 71/2, and required a good deal of my time. Like most children, they were eager to participate in many activities. But good diabetes management also takes time: time to test, evaluate, inject, and, of course, eat! (Have you ever noticed how many extracurricular activities coincide with meal times?) During that first year of insulin injections, my children had to taste a few almonds: They participated in no extra activities—that was the only way I could cope.

Since then, I have switched to multiple injections. I now have greater flexibility, and my children have extra activities again. Gradually, I am developing a new sense of normalcy. I have learned that living with diabetes can still include old passions such as cross-country skiing and playing and teaching the violin. Diabetes has also inspired me to see some old pastimes and chores in a new light. I love to cook, and my new knowledge about good nutrition and food choices is helping me to create a cookbook.

Still, my greatest challenge is balancing my

responsibilities. I know that better blood glucose control will help reduce my chances of developing complications. But tight control robs me of spontaneity and it can prove dangerous when I have to deal with the sudden changes and altered plans that are part of life with children. My dilemma is that I would like to ensure that I will be around to enjoy grandchildren, and yet I want to be a full participant in life now.

Although my life with diabetes does seem full of almonds, there are some raisins too. Life tastes sweet indeed, when every Halloween my children set aside some of their sweets for "Mommy's Emergency Kit," or when my youngest daughter bakes an imaginary chocolate cake "with no sugar." My family has learned how to respond and help me when my blood sugars are low, and not to be offended by my behavior when my blood sugars are too high. Everyone now understands why I must carry a purse that resembles a well-stocked pantry.

As living proof of my mother's old bittersweet saying, the members of my family—who can't always come first—keep finding more raisins to offer me. And do they ever taste sweet.

-Evelyne Pytka

I Saw My Future

A good friend of mine called one night in need of advice. She said she'd been feeling bad about herself lately, even taking anti-depressant pills, but she still felt like she couldn't go on. "You've been depressed before," she said to me, "How did you pull out of it?"

I paused. She was referring to my late teen years. Back then, I took all the frustration and anxiety of young adulthood, of my parents' separation, and of maintaining a straight-A average in school out on my health. With all that was going on, I had no time to take care of my diabetes.

How did I do it then, when my blood sugars were consistently higher than my meter could measure and my energy level barely enough to get me off the couch to the bathroom every hour? What got me through the times when, at 19, I felt that I had nothing to live for, that I didn't deserve good health, that I wasn't worth the effort of trying, that I may as well give up?

She was right. I once did fall into a pit of anger, fear, guilt, and depression, and I had to get myself out.

"I guess I saw my future," I told her. "And it wasn't that great."

"What do you mean?" she asked.

"I knew where my behavior was leading me. And I knew I could change it. So I pictured myself, years into the future, how I wanted to be. Everything. What I would look like, what I'd be doing, who I'd be with. I created my ideal self. And then I had something to look forward to."

The silence grew long as she was thinking. "If that fails," I said, "I usually go shopping."

"You're right," she said, laughing. "Look how well you've done. You did have something to look forward to. And it all began with setting your mind to do it."

We hung up, and I just sat for a long time. I couldn't remember a day since I was 7 years old when I didn't think about my diabetes, what I was up against, and what my future held.

I have had to "pull myself out" many times, with every unintentional ice cream binge, every higher-than-we-like-it A1C result, every new complication and drop in self-esteem. I might have deserved an A for effort, but I'd still feel like I'd flunked.

I remember the question, "What motivates you?" coming up in a diabetes support group session that I attended. What surprised me most that night wasn't that everyone gave the same answer, but that every woman in the room said she was motivated by one thing: fear. Fear of blindness, fear of death, fear of mystery and of uncertainty, and of their own bodies.

I realized then how important is the motivation that gets us to take care of diabetes. Most people, at some point in their lives, will claim they're dieting or getting in shape, but usually the goal is short-term, like a high school reunion or a desirable number on the scale.

But diabetes is a daily disease—blood tests, shots, walks, meals of specific size at specific times—on an infinite time line. Years, decades, forever. It takes something very powerful to keep you motivated for that.

I generally don't perform well under negative reinforcement. The night those seven women admitted that fear was what motivated them, I kept trying to picture myself running for my life, trying to escape from the perils of diabetes. But I knew I wouldn't keep up my daily routine that way, with the Cloud of Doom hanging over my head. I had better things to do.

I chose, instead, to picture my future, imagining myself as attractive, healthy, happy, and successful. Then I could run to something, rather than from something. The world didn't look so frightful. And I could focus my energies in positive ways. I believed in myself.

Eventually, my parents sorted out their problems and went on, and I graduated from college with an A-average. I've also met a doctor who gives me posititve encouragement and exceptional attention in controlling my diabetes. (Not that I have perfect control, of course, but my doctor and I have become weekly comrades in an effort to make the highs less high and the lows less frequent.)

Now, every so often, when I find myself drifting from my normally strict regimen and wishing I could crawl into a hole and hide from my diabetes, I think about my friend and that phone call. Then I look at how my future is turning out—what I look like, what I'm doing, and who I'm with. I am strenghtened to see how far I have come. And I have high hopes for the future.

-Karen Schulz

What Needles Me About Having Diabetes

"Do you have to give yourself shots?"
"Yeah."
"Where?"
"Usually in my arm, leg, or stomach."
"Your stomach???? Doesn't it hurt?"
"Well, sometimes it does, when I hit a sore muscle or a blood vessel."
"I could never give myself a shot in the stomach. I'd pass out."

Since I was diagnosed with diabetes more than six years ago, I have engaged in this conversation countless times. You know, diabetes gives me some really challenging things to do like eat a special diet, constantly monitor my blood sugars, and lead a life that is rather controlled. But this conversation sums up the typical reaction I get whenever I tell people that I have diabetes.

When people say that they could never give themselves shots, sometimes I think they aren't listening to themselves. Although some seem pretty impressed that this has become as routine for me as brushing my teeth, others, by the looks on their faces, have a mental image of a 4-inch needle as thick as a pencil that I have to stick in my body. They don't want to know any more.

Besides, everyone does things to stay healthy. This is one of the things I do to stay healthy. Don't people realize that not injecting myself would be really irresponsible? If they actually had diabetes, would they really rather suffer uncontrolled diabetes with dry-as-cotton mouth, endless trips to the bathroom, plummeting weight, fatigue—and those are just the fun parts—or would they administer those injections just like I do?

Most people mean well, I know, but hearing the same thing over and over again can get old. For once, I would love to be asked if there are other ways I control the disease, like diet or exercise. Why does everyone focus on needles and shots? Isn't anyone impressed that I can control a disease like diabetes? And still lead a somewhat normal life for a 23-year-old woman?

Most people don't know I have diabetes until they offer me a piece of candy, a cookie, or a piece of gum. My question: "Is it sugar-free?"

"Dieting?" they ask.

"Nope," I say, "I have diabetes." Then we do the shot routine. And after that, most people go on to declare that they simply Would Not Survive if they were denied their daily candy bar, and how can I stand not eating candy?

This is the other thing people seem to know about diabetes. I explain that I can eat candy, but only when my blood sugar is low, not just when I have a craving. (Many times—especially if the person has an obvious weight problem—I would love to answer, "I'm glad I have to watch my diet and exercise, you might want to try it yourself.")

I know it's hard for anyone who doesn't have diabetes to know how it feels, but it might help if everyone knew just a little more about it.

I have been controlling this disease for a few years with some success. But when I'm at home, my parents seem to want to make my disease theirs. When dinner is being prepared, someone will say, "Don't forget to take your shot, Sally." Right. Glad you reminded me, but it's not something that is likely to slip my mind. (Sharing this disease is a tricky process.)

Thanks to my parents, I have a library of books about diabetes and a lifetime membership to the American Diabetes Association. I have all the information I need at my fingertips, and I want to share it.

I know that most people—even my parents— are curious, and things like shots are unfamiliar to them, so they ask questions. The problem is no one ever comes up with new ones.

I have yet to encounter an original response to the news that I have diabetes. Maybe I should start the ball rolling and say something positive to the next person I meet who has diabetes. If what goes around comes around, someday I may finally hear someone say, "You have diabetes? Is that why you're in such great shape?"

-Sally A. Hedman

At Home On The Range

A little over 100 years ago, I wouldn't have been here herding cows from the back of a horse. Number one, I'm a woman. Number two, I have type I diabetes. That would have cut my life short, male or female!

My husband and I lease a large cow outfit in the Missouri Breaks of Montana and punch cattle on it. Our ranch is surrounded by reminders of the past: a grave of a man killed by Indians; two early forts that offered protection to the trappers, settlers, and the steamboats that came up the Missouri River; and an old saloon just over the hill at the mouth of Dog Creek where early-day cowboys had hell-raisin' times. This was where hundreds of thousands of cattle were pushed north across the Missouri to fresh range in the Milk River country.

Even today, the only way to get around our ranch is on horseback, in all types of weather, fording the Judith River that bisects our ranch. We cannot eat or even sleep according to nature's plan for gentler folks.

Eight years ago, I was on an elk hunting trip in the Beartooth Mountains. I had to keep getting out of my tent at night, despite a howling snowstorm, to relieve myself. I was so thirsty I kept a canteen of water in my bedroll so it wouldn't freeze. If I had been in the Sahara Desert, instead of the frozen, Montana mountain country, I couldn't have felt thirstier.

The only thing that saved me from ketoacidosis, I believe, was all the exercise I got trucking up and down mountainsides and cutting piles of wood for the fire. When we rode back into town, I went to see the saw-bones.

Then I was glad it was 1983 instead of 1883. I didn't go to the hospital, but I took a week-long course in diabetes management. I got myself one of those new-fangled blood glucose meters, and I started giving myself shots. I read books on diabetes management and came across one that described how to mimic the action of a normal pancreas with multiple injections.

My lifestyle, you see, just didn't fit the timetable

that my diabetes routine dictated. I didn't want to give up any of my cowgirl life, so with my doctor's approval, I switched to multiple injections. I felt as though I had been released from the crow-bar motel! My blood sugar normalized, and I realized that I could rein in the diabetes and retake control of my life.

I am still where I love to be, out in the big sky country. And big sky country in my family means cattle, horses, and range. The things I do daily take me far from home and modern civilization. Horses and cows have changed little since the 1870s.

Every spring we gather all the mother cows off the windswept winter range and put them in large pastures to calve. We ride these pastures every day to make sure all is going well. March in Montana is not really spring and in snow and cold the little calves are born.

After calving comes branding. All of the family and friends come to help, so branding becomes a social, as well as hard-working, time of the year.

In summer, we drive the cows and calves to new pastures. We ride out to find strays and to help any sick critters. This can get pretty exciting in tough country, when my horse is going lickety-split after a doggie who sure doesn't act sick! With ropes twirling, we "head and heel" the animal. The we can give a shot or a pill.

In the fall we gather again to round up the cattle and count them. It takes many rides to dig them all out of the hills. The calves are weaned from their mothers and shipped to town. The cows are put out to winter pasture, so they can be fed in bad weather. We use a team of draft horses and a pickup. It sometimes takes all day to get them fed in a Montana blizzard. By spring the cycle begins again.

We break our own horses. My husband can "ride

anything with hair" as they say of bronco twisters, and I can hold my own. It takes a string of six horses for each of us to keep from being "footback." Most days we ride more than 15 miles.

Cowgirl or not, I still have to pack my meter, strips, and a meal along in my saddle bags. I go to the doctor "pretty regular." My glycosylated hemoglobin level (A_{1C}) is normal and I have had no complications. I try to eat my good lean beef with complex carbohydrates, and every now and then I even have a piece of pie at the family gatherings.

I guess my point is that even though I live my life happy in the free-wheelin' style of the past, the present and future are mine because of modern medical advances.

-Jackie A. Holmgren

I'm No Fred Astaire

Most of the time, I feel like Fred Astaire. It may look easy to live with diabetes, but it's a lot of hard work behind the scenes.

If someone asks me what it's like to live with diabetes, I laugh. To the uninitiated, the daily regimen of blood testing, insulin juggling, Exchanges, and exercise is mind-boggling. They don't know, and I can't tell them, how many steps there are in this dance. Diabetes sneakily affects virtually all aspects of my life.

I got insulin-dependent diabetes at age 25. I am 31 now, and strangely enough, I only vaguely remember what my life was like before the choreography got so complicated. (What person with diabetes doesn't automatically convert Haagen-Dazs into exchanges?)

Getting diabetes in my mid-twenties was both devastating and well-timed. At that age, I could think of myself as a "person" with diabetes, but what made it particularly hard was how long it took me to gain some control. I was an avid exerciser and oat bran devotee, pre-diabetes. Well sure, I thought, I just have to eat right, work out, take a little insulin (snap my fingers, click my heels), and I'll be fine. None of those nasty complications for me in the future.

But that didn't happen. My blood sugars shot up high, then swooped down. I got depressed. I felt very, very old and sick, and I took more and more shots daily. My only cheery memories of those first few years are from my "honeymoon period," which lasted an unbelievable 12 months.

Unfortunately, the honeymoon had to end. Frustrated with the jerky rhythms of the three-shot-a-day routine, I turned to the insulin pump. With scenes from the Bionic Woman in my head and the gloomy belief that I would never wear a bikini again, I decided to give it a try.

It certainly wasn't love at first sight. It was hard to convince myself that wearing a needle in my stomach was a wonderful and enviable thing. And the plastic paraphernalia that came with the pump kindled no spark of joy within either.

The pump opened up a whole new world for me, however, in the lingerie department. For instance, how to wear an object the size of a deck of cards somewhere in my clothing where it wouldn't be mistaken for a walkie-talkie? Excuse me lady, your beeper seems to have fallen into your pantyhose. Luckily for me, panty girdles hadn't gone the way of 1950s movies, but many saleswomen questioned my need for tummy-flattening panels in a size 6.

Then there were the delicately phrased locker-room questions. Not needing any insulin while I am exercising, I would put the pump in my purse and allow the tubing to swish behind me. There were tactful comments about how I seemed to have gotten something stuck to myself in the shower (a common occurrence, I know). And subtle, sensitive questions like, "What in God's name is that in your stomach?"

Using a blood glucose monitor also requires a steely nerve. There was the time I was nearly arrested in the Senate visitors' gallery. Working late one evening, I recklessly pulled out my meter to check my blood sugar. Vigilant security agents thought I had sneaked in a tape recorder.

Pleading that I had diabetes, I endured long minutes of hissed reprimands as the agent interrogated me. I tried to ignore the bevy of security agents, complete with earphones, who had promptly appeared to monitor my suspicious behavior.

Years later, my machines continue to set the tempo for my waltz with diabetes. I still don't have perfect control. My blood sugars frequently look like temperature readings on Mars, but the pump has given me flexibility and a more normal life.

The diabetes is better, too. I don't spend time thinking about complications so much as I worry about the fat content of cashews and the amount of insulin I'll need to cover a late dinner out. I could never have reached this point without the support—which falls somewhere between breezy acceptance and total frustration—of my husband and family.

I keep abreast of the latest research (if I can understand it), hit the exercise club, eat three square meals a day, and carry a well-stocked purse the size of a refrigerator. Friends tell me I make it look easy, but I'm still no Fred Astaire.

-Susan L. Hildebrandt

Twenty Years and Counting

My favorite T-shirt is old, worn, and unraveling around the edges. It's comfortably shabby now—and it's been on my mind a lot. Powdermilk Biscuits is emblazoned on the front. Anyone familiar with the radio show "Prairie Home Companion" and the mythical town of Lake Wobegone, knows about powdermilk biscuits. They are a most important part of life there, because they "give you the strength to do what needs to be done."

I have lived 20 years with insulin-dependent diabetes and what has had to be done is four shots of insulin and two blood tests a day. It requires vigilance 24 hours a day. Although I have, at times, felt triumphant—ready to "leap tall buildings with a single bound," other times I've felt like I was carrying a huge burden uphill. I have needed those powdermilk biscuits.

I was introduced to injections and diet by a physician who believed that if you don't make a big deal out of it, then it won't be a big deal. He sat me down in his office and told me that I'd have to take a shot every day. He filled the syringe, pointed to my leg, and said, "Just a quick jab. That's all there is to it." And I believed him.

Then he tore off a diet from a pad, handed it to me, and told me to follow it. That was it. No big deal.

I went home. My mother cried when she heard the news, but my tears came gradually, with each insulin reaction, each time I felt lousy, each time I felt what "no big deal" was.

In six months, I was off to college and my control "roller coastered." My weight skyrocketed on the 2,200-calorie diet the doctor gave me. I was a regular at the emergency room. And most alarmingly, I discovered the negative attitudes some people harbor about diabetes.

In the third year following my diagnosis, I chose to write a paper for a nutrition class. I wanted to find out how students with diabetes were managing with the food served in the dining halls. Much to my surprise, I couldn't locate anyone with diabetes on campus. Because of confidentiality concerns, health services wouldn't release any names to me. So I worked by word of mouth.

One woman I contacted hurried me to her room, closed the door, and made it very clear she wanted no one to know of her diabetes. It would, she was sure, affect friendships and her whole future. I didn't understand her attitude. I didn't believe that diabetes was like leprosy, so my friends didn't treat me like it was. Looking back, I realize that my family and friends have been my powdermilk biscuits from the beginning.

When I began injecting myself with insulin, I used a glass syringe with disposable needles. I tested my urine for sugar with tape and for ketones with a fizzing tablet. I took one shot of insulin a day that tied me to rigid mealtimes. The few articles I could find to read on diabetes were dull and somber.

Each new year, however, has brought new developments that have profoundly affected my life. Disposable syringes, improved quality insulins, normalization of the diabetic diet, and glucose self-monitoring (the best biscuit since sliced bread), have all lightened my burden.

But even though diabetes has been gentle with me, I still feel as tattered as my T-shirt. Although I have the advantage of being a dietitian and having access to good medical care, my knowledge doesn't always translate into good choices. Knowing the exchange system inside out just causes a huge guilt trip when I don't do the right thing. Knowing isn't doing, and it's the doing that makes me tired.

So at this 20-year mark I have been forced to admit to myself and others how weary I am of diabetes. Every time I do, I feel better. It's like I've gotten a biscuit every time someone else understands, on some level, what it means to have diabetes.

To my great surprise, my honest expression of need has resulted in a generous showing of support. Two friends treated me to a 20-year celebration, with dinner, poems, special gifts, and a trip to the theater to show their friendship and solidarity with me. In this loving celebration, they created a ritual of real sharing.

Funny, my burden is still there. I know all that I have to do. But I think I have found a fresh supply of those powdermilk biscuits.

-Barbara Ryan

We're Only Human

Do you feel out of control with food? So did I. I was diagnosed with type I diabetes when I was nine. I'm 24 now. I remember feeling guilty—had I caused this by eating too much sugar? That's what my friends said.

Mom told me I couldn't eat sugar anymore. Telling that to a nine-year-old child is like telling the sun not to shine. I started eating twice as much candy as I ever did before I was diagnosed. I would go to the drugstore at lunchtime and buy candy with all the other fourth graders and hide it in my desk at school. I could be "bad" and nobody knew—except my doctor.

"You're the worst diabetic in the clinic," she told me when my 24-hour urine results came back sky-high. (This was in the days before glycohemoglobin testing.) "You're such a smart girl, you should be doing much better."

Years later, I would ask myself what that meant. Was I so smart that I shouldn't have wanted to eat candy like all the other kids? Are "smart" kids not supposed to get upset when they are told they will have to take shots every day for the rest of their lives? Did being smart and having diabetes mean I was now supposed to be perfect?

I developed a food problem in high school. At the beginning, of each school year, I would get stressed out, overeat, and gain about 10 pounds. Around January, I would calm down a little, realize that I was capable of getting straight A's, then try to become "perfect" with food as well. I would rigidly monitor everything that went into my mouth, and would forbid myself blood sugars above 180.

Every time I slipped, I would get depressed and vow to be "good" again the next day. The 10 pounds would come off, but I still was never totally happy with myself.

College was much worse. I went to a very tough, competitive university where everyone had been a straight "A" student in high school. I was no longer the smartest—in fact, most of my grades were below average, something I was definitely not used to and was completely unable to cope with.

I began to binge-eat constantly. I couldn't read or study without eating and would keep eating until I was stuffed. Physical hunger had nothing to do with it. I was completely out of control and hated myself for it.

Fortunately (although I didn't see it that way then), I was never able to make myself throw up all the excess food as some other women I knew were doing. Instead, I gained 40 pounds over four years of college.

I was caught in a terrible cycle—I felt bad about

myself as a person. To make myself feel better, I ate. This only made me feel worse afterward, so the cycle continued.

I saw a psychologist after my disastrous sophomore year. It took a while, but he taught me to do something very simple: Replace the word "bad" with "human." Makes a big difference, doesn't it?

I realized that I had not been allowing myself to have faults—to be human. I thought that any time my blood sugar went up, I was a "bad" diabetic," and maybe even deserved to have complications.

The truth is, there is not one person with diabetes who always has blood sugars in the normal range. Blood sugars will fluctuate with illness, stress, or a change in schedule; it's not humanly possible to be in control all the time, and it can be harmful to think that it is.

Also, most people—including those of us with diabetes—like the taste of candy and other sugary and fatty foods, right? I've learned to limit the amount of these foods that I eat, but I no longer feel guilty for wanting them. I'd be pretty strange if I didn't.

I've learned to do my best at sticking to my diet, exercising, and keeping my blood sugar as close to normal as possible, but to forgive myself if I slip. These things happen.

I've also learned that I haven't failed if I call my doctor when I have a problem. Diabetes is a tough disease for any person to handle, and nobody can or should do it alone. We must take control of the day-to-day management of the disease, but when problems arise, it's time to ask for help from people trained to do just that.

I no longer judge myself by how much I eat. Although I've lost the weight I gained, I've learned that I'm not "bad" if I gain a pound or if my blood sugar is high, any more than I'm "good" if I starve myself and end up having a reaction. I am who I am regardless of what the scale says, what the glucose meter says, or for that matter, what any other person says!

-Miriam E. Tucker

Appendix

How-To's

How to Self-Monitor Your Blood Glucose

Follow your meter manufacturer's instructions for best results. If you have problems, there should be an 800 number in the printed instructions that you can call for help.

Equipment:
+ Lancet (blood-letting device)
+ Clean test strip
+ Cotton ball or tissue
+ A watch or other timing device
+ A blood glucose meter or color chart for matching

1. Make sure your hands are clean and dry. Soap or lotion on your hands can cause incorrect test results.
2. Puncture the skin of a finger, toe, or earlobe with the lancet. Most people use the side of a finger.
3. Squeeze out a large drop of blood.
4. Place the blood drop on the pad of a test strip (or onto the sensor if your meter already has the test strip inside it). Wait the instructed amount of time for the test strip to develop.
5. Wipe excess blood from the test strip, if manufacturer's instructions say to. Then insert the test strip into the meter or compare the test strip to the chart on the vial. (With some meters, it is not necessary to wipe off the blood and a smaller drop of blood will do.)

6. Dispose of the lancet safely with your syringe needles.
7. Record your numbers.

How to Test for Ketones

Perform this test to check for ketones in the urine if:
a blood glucose test is 250 mg/dl or higher, or
a urine glucose test shows 1/2% or higher.
Equipment:
✦Ketone test strip
✦Cup or clean container for sample
✦A watch or other timing device
1. Dip a ketone test strip in a urine sample, or pass it through the stream of urine.
2. Time test according to the directions on the package.
3. The strip will change colors if ketones are present. Compare test strip to package color chart.
4. Record the results.

How to Prepare an Insulin Injection

Equipment:
✦sterile syringe
✦bottle of insulin
✦alcohol swab, if desired, to clean the injection site or the insulin bottle
1. Wash hands.
2. Choose injection site.
3. Roll the bottle of insulin between your hands. (Regular insulin doesn't need to be rolled.) Don't shake it, because this makes air bubbles in the insulin. Air bubbles interfere with correct measurement of the units of insulin.
4. If desired, wipe the top of the bottle with an alcohol swab, then let the alcohol dry completely. Don't blow on it to dry it more quickly.

5. Holding the syringe with the needle pointing up, draw air into it by pulling down on the plunger to the amount that matches your insulin dose.
6. Remove the cap from the needle. Hold the insulin bottle steady on a table top, and push the needle straight down into the rubber top on the bottle. Push down on the plunger to inject the air into the insulin bottle.
7. Leave the needle in the bottle and the plunger pushed all the way in while you pick up the bottle and turn it upside down. The point of the needle should be covered by the insulin.
8. Pull the correct amount of insulin into the syringe by pulling back on the plunger.
9. Check for air bubbles on the inside of the syringe. If you see air bubbles, keep the bottle upside down and push the plunger up so the insulin goes back into the bottle.
10. Pull down on the plunger to refill the syringe. If necessary, empty and refill until all air bubbles in the syringe are gone.
11. Remove the needle from the bottle after checking again that you have the correct dose.
12. If you need to set the syringe down before giving your injection, recap and lay it on its side. Make sure the needle doesn't touch anything.

How to Mix Insulins
Equipment:
    ✦Sterile disposable syringe, the correct size for the total units of insulin
    ✦Bottles of insulin
    ✦Alcohol swab, if desired, to clean the injection site or the insulin bottle
1. Be clear on the amounts of each insulin and the total units you want. To find the total units, add

the units of short-acting insulin to the units of intermediate- or long-acting insulin.
2. Wash your hands.
3. Roll any bottle of cloudy intermediate- or long-acting insulin between your hands. Don't shake it because this makes air bubbles in the insulin.
4. Draw air into the syringe equal to intermediate- or long-acting dose.
5. With the bottle upright on a table, inject the air into that bottle. Take out the needle without removing any insulin.
6. Draw air into the syringe equal to the dose of short-acting insulin and inject the air into the upright bottle of short-acting insulin.
7. With the needle still in the short-action insulin bottle, turn it upside down so that insulin covers the top of the needle.
8. Check for air bubbles on the inside of the syringe. If you see air bubbles, keep the bottle upside down and push the plunger up so the insulin goes back into the bottle.
9. Pull the correct amount of insulin into the syringe by pulling back on the plunger. If necessary, empty and refill until all air bubbles in the syringe are gone. Remove the syringe.
10. With the bottle of intermediate- or long-acting insulin held upside down, insert the syringe. (You have already injected the right amount of air into this bottle.)
11. Slowly pull the plunger down to draw in the right dosage of intermediate- or long-acting insulin. This will be the total units of the short and intermediate- or long- acting insulins.
12. Do not return any extra insulin back to this bottle. It's now a mixture. Double check for the correct total amount of insulin. If incorrect, discard the syringe contents and start over.

13. Take the needle out of the bottle, recap, and lay the syringe carefully on a table without it touching anything.

How to Store Mixed Insulins

1. Only mix insulins made by the same company. For instance, don't mix Regular made by Lilly with NPH made by NovoNordisk.
2. If the mixture of insulin is stored in a glass or a plastic syringe, it will remain stable for 21 days under refrigeration.
3. Keep the prefilled syringes capped and in a vertical or oblique position with the needle pointing upward to avoid plugging problems.
4. Before injection, the plunger should be pulled back a little and the syringe tipped back and forth a few times to remix the insulin. Carefully push the plunger back to its original position, pushing air out of the syringe but not insulin.
5. NPH and Regular insulins that are premixed by a manufacturer or that are mixed by you are stable and can be stored like any other insulin. There is no difference in action between a stored NPH-Regular mixture and a fresh one.
6. Mixture of Regular and Lente insulins is not recommended except for patients already adequately controlled on such a mixture. The Lente insulin delays the onset of action of the Regular insulin in an unpredictable way. If Regular-Lente mixtures are to be used, always store the mixture for the same length of time each day.

How to Inject Insulin

Equipment:
✦prepared filled sterile syringe
✦sterile cotton ball or gauze square, if desired, to cover the injection site for a few seconds after the injection

1. Choose an injection site with fatty tissue, such as the backs of the arms, the top and outside of the thighs, the abdomen except for a 1-inch square around the belly button, or the buttocks. Make sure the site and your hands are clean.
2. Gently pinch a fold of skin between your thumb and forefinger and inject straight in if you have a normal amount of fatty tissue. For a thin adult or a small child, you may inject on a 45-degree angle.
3. Push the needle through the skin as quickly as you can.
4. After the needle is in, do a blood vessel check by drawing back on the plunger slightly. If blood appears, remove the needle and find a new site. When you are sure you are not injecting into a blood vessel, push the plunger in to inject the insulin.
5. Pull the needle straight out.
6. Cover the injection site with your finger or a dry cotton ball or gauze and apply slight pressure for 5 to 8 seconds—but do not rub. Rubbing may spread the insulin too quickly or irritate your skin.
7. Write down how much insulin you injected, the time of day, and the site you chose.

How to Reuse Your Syringe

1. Carefully recap the syringe when you aren't using it.
2. Don't let the needle touch anything but clean skin and your insulin bottle stopper. If it touches anything else, don't reuse it.
3. Store the used syringe at room temperature.
4. There will always be a tiny, even invisible, amount of insulin left in the syringe. So use one syringe with just one type of insulin to avoiding mixing insulins. For this reason, reusing syringes in which you have mixed insulins is not recommended.
5. Do not reuse a needle that is bent or dull. However, just because an injection is painful doesn't mean the needle is dull. You may have hit a nerve ending or have wet alcohol on your skin, if you use alcohol to clean the injection site.
6. Do not wipe your needle with alcohol. This removes some of the coating that makes the needle go more smoothly into your skin.
7. When you're finished with a syringe, dispose of it properly according to the laws in your area. Contact the city or county sanitation department for information.

What to Teach Others About Mixing and Injecting Glucagon

1. A glucagon kit has a syringe filled with diluting fluid and a bottle of powdered glucagon. You must mix the diluting fluid with the powder before it can be injected. The instructions for mixing and injecting glucagon are included in the kit.

2. Inject glucagon in the same way and in the same parts of the body that you inject insulin.

3. If glucagon is mixed in a syringe but not used, you may refrigerate the capped syringe and use it for up to 30 days.

4. The person with low blood glucose should respond to the glucagon injection in 15 to 30 minutes. If not, call emergency personnel.

5. The person will likely feel nauseated or vomit. So, keep the head elevated.

6. As soon as the person can swallow, offer regular soda, crackers, or toast.

7. Then offer a sandwich or protein snack.

8. Check blood glucose.

Resources

For People With Type I Diabetes

Books on Self-Care

From the American Diabetes Association:
To order see order form at the end of the Resources.

The Fitness Book: For People With Diabetes
Begin your very own exercise program with the knowledge of a fitness expert. Already exercising? The Fitness Book will help add variety to your program. Just a few of the topics: how exercise helps you lose weight, the myths about dieting, why all people with diabetes should exercise, how to exercise safely, much more.

You'll learn that staying fit doesn't have to take all your time, sweat, and tears. All it takes is the motivation and expert information you'll find in The Fitness Book. 149 pages. Softcover. #CSMFB
Nonmember: $18.95
Member: $14.95

Necessary Toughness
Join Kansas City Chiefs star Jonathan Hayes as he learns to tackle life with diabetes. His story is an encouraging journey through the rigors of successfully managing a pro football career and diabetes.

Jonathan's discipline and attention to self care will make you want to tackle your diabetes, too. 116 pages. Softcover. #CGFNT
Nonmember: $7.95
Member: $6.25

Diabetes A to Z
Weave your way through the jungle of difficult diabetes terms with our dictionary-style guidebook. Answers to questions about lifestyle, nutrition, exercise, and much more are presented in clear, simple terms. Alphabetized format allows you to refer to everything from Adolescence to Exchange Lists in a snap. 104 pages. Softcover. #CGFDAZ
Nonmember: $9.95
Member: $7.95

Diabetes: A Positive Approach—Video
Pop this award-winning video into your VCR and you'll be on your way to Hollywood and to making diabetes a positive part of your life. Comedian Tom Parks and other celebrities will make you laugh as you learn about diet, fitness, insulin adjustment, pregnancy, oral medication, and more. VHS only. #CVIDPOS
Nonmember: $19.95
Member: $17.95

Diabetes & Pregnancy: What to Expect
"I have diabetes, but I want to have a baby. How can I assure myself a successful pregnancy?" Learn how in this comprehensive guide for women with type I diabetes. The specifics are covered in detail: the stages of an unborn baby's development, tests to expect, labor and delivery, birth control, and much more. 70 pages. Softcover. #CPREDP
Nonmember: $9.95
Member: $7.95

Buyer's Guide to Diabetes Products
Compare features from different manufacturers of insulin, syringes, jet injectors, pumps, test strips, monitors, and more. Don't go shopping without it. Updated yearly. 42 pages. Softcover. #CMISBUY
Nonmember: $2.95
Member: $2.65

Menu Planners and Cookbooks

Month of Meals
Just because it's a holiday doesn't mean you can't enjoy delicious food. A "Special Occasion" section offers tips for brunches, holidays, parties, and restaurants to give you delicious dining options in most any setting. Menu choices include Chicken Cacciatore, Oven Fried Fish, Sloppy Joes, Crab Cakes, many others. 57 pages. Spiral-bound. #CMP-MOM
Nonmember: $12.50
Member: $9.95

Month of Meals 2
A healthy diet doesn't have to keep you from enjoying your favorite restaurants. Tips and meal suggestions for Mexican, Italian, and Chinese restaurants are featured. Quick-to-fix and ethnic recipes are also included. Menu choices include Beef Burritos, Chop Suey, Veal Piccata, Stuffed Peppers, many others. 64 pages. Spiral-bound. #CMPMOM2
Nonmember: $12.50
Member: $9.95

Month of Meals 3
Enjoy fast food without the guilt—Month of Meals 3 shows you how. Choose from McDonald's, Wendy's, Taco Bell, Kentucky Fried Chicken, many others. Special sections offer valuable tips: how to read ingre-

dient labels on packages; how to prepare meals for picnics & barbeques; how to plan meals when you're ill; more. Spiral-bound. #CMPMOM3
Nonmember: $12.50
Member: $9.95

Month of Meals 4
Beef up your meal planning with old-time family favorites like Meatloaf, Pot Roast, Oven Crispy Chicken, Beef Stroganoff, many others. Hints for turning family-size meals into delicious left-overs will keep those generous portions from going to waste. Meal plans for one or two people are also featured. 74 pages. Spiral-bound. #CMPMOM4
Nonmember: $12.50
Member: $9.95

Month of Meals 5
A month's worth of fresh new menu choices with a special focus on vegetarian selections. Choose from Pumpkin Apple Muffins, Oklahoma Bean Salad, Oven-Baked Tofu, Stuffed Zucchini, Sauteed Kale and Onion, Eggplant Italian, Cucumbers with Dill Dressing, many others. Spiral-bound. #CMPMOM5
Nonmember: $12.50
Member: $9.95

The Healthy HomeStyle Cookbook
More than 150 recipes, each low in fat, cholesterol, sugar, and calories. Try Dutch Apple Pancakes, Sweet and Sour Meatballs, Chicken Nuggets, Sloppy Joes, and others. Energy- and time-saving tips for microwaving and freezing, plus ideas for cutting fat and calories are featured. Special "lay-flat" binding allows hands-free reference to your favorite recipes. 192 pages. Softcover. #CCBHHS
Nonmember: $12.50
Member: $9.95

Holiday Cookbook
Holidays mean delicious food, even on a healthy diet. From Eggnog to Cranberry Rolls, our Holiday Cookbook will fill your table with tempting recipes from traditional Thanksgiving, Christmas, and Hanukkah feasts to savory meals for any occasion. 219 pages. Hardcover. #CCBH
Nonmember: $19.95
Member: $17.95

Special Celebrations and Parties Cookbook
Cheesecake? Brownies? On MY diet? Yes! Whether it's a Fourth of July barbecue, Mother's Day brunch, or birthday bash, you'll find an irresistible temptation on every page. 256 pages. Hardcover. #CCBSCP
Nonmember: $19.95
Member: $17.95

Family Cookbook, Volume I
More than 250 recipes—from Chinese Ginger Chicken to Strawberry Shortcake, each inexpensive to prepare and delicious to eat. An encyclopedia of nutrition information, tips on eating out, brown-bagging, weight control, and exercise are featured. 388 pages. Hardcover. #CCBF1
Nonmember: $23.00
Member: $20.70

Family Cookbook, Volume II
Includes ways to cut sugar, calories, and costs—plus more than 250 unforgettable recipes: Texas-Style Barbeque Sauce, Veal Cutlets, and more. An entire section is devoted to living with diabetes and gives advice on the emotional aspects of dieting. 452 pages. Hardcover. #CCBF2
Nonmember: $23.00
Member: $20.70

Family Cookbook, Volume III
Add more than 200 recipes to your treasury—Broiled Scallops, Lobster Tails, and others. Included are tips on microwaving, food processing, and freezing for fix-ahead meals. Recipes from various ethnic cuisines are included. 434 pages. Hardcover. #CCBF3
Nonmember: $23.00
Member: 20.70

Family Cookbook, Volume IV
Recipes from Boston Scrod to Santa Fe Chicken (more than 200 in all) fill each page with great American flavor. Features recipes for appetizers, soups, salads, breads, meats, poultry, fish, vegetables, desserts, and more. A colorful introductory section features tidbits about the history of American cuisine. 403 pages. Hardcover. #CCBF4
Nonmember: $23.00
Member: $20.70

Exchange Lists for Meal Planning
Colorful charts, helpful tips on good nutrition, and an introduction to the six easy-to-use food Exchange Lists show you how to balance your diet and gain control over diabetes. (Also available in large print.) Softcover. #CELMP
Nonmember: $1.30
Member: $1.10

Reading Food Labels: A Handbood for People With Diabetes
An interactive guide to gathering all the information you can from the Nutrition Facts on food labels. 16 pages. #CMISRFL
Nonmember: $0.75
Member: $0.60

From Other Publishers:

Fast Food Facts by Marion J. Franz, RD, MS (DCI/CHRONIMED Publishing, PO Box 47945, Minneapolis, MN 55447; 1990) Nutritive and Exchange values for fast food restaurants. #CDSFFF
Nonmember: $6.95
Member: $6.25

Convenience Food Facts by Arlene Monk, RD, CDE, and Marion J. Franz, RD, MS (DCI/CHRONIMED Publishing, PO Box 47945, Minneapolis, MN 55447; 1991) Nutritive and Exchange values for grocery store items by brand name. #CDSDFF
Nonmember: $10.95
Member: $9.85

Exchanges for All Occasions by Marion J. Franz, RD, MS (DCI/CHRONIMED Publishing, PO Box 47945, Minneapolis, MN 55447; 1987) Nutritive and Exchange values for everyday foods. #CDSEXCH
Nonmember: $12.95
Member: $11.65

Eat for Life: The Food and Nutrition Board's Guide to Reducing Your Risk of Chronic Disease Catherine E. Woteki, PhD, RD, and Paul R. Thomas, EdD, RD (Editors) (National Academy Press, 2101 Constitution Avenue, NW, PO Box 285, Washington, DC 20055; 1992) Easy-to-understand version of National Academy of Sciences nutrition guidelines for good health. #CDSEFL
Nonmember: $18.95
Member: $17.05

Service and Support Groups

Membership in the American Diabetes Association

ADA's members-only magazine, *Diabetes Forecast*, helps you better understand and control your diabetes, so you enjoy more of the good things in life. Each month, *Diabetes Forecast* is filled with updates on advances in diabetes research, treatment, and easier self-care, advice on coping with daily stress, information on safe ways to exercise, and delicious easy-to-fix recipes. Introduce yourself to others who share your concerns and also live with the challenge of diabetes.

Diabetes Forecast in one of the many benefits of ADA membership. To receive more information on membership in the ADA, call (800) 232-3472, ext. 343 for membership services.

Although your best resource for information is likely to be your local ADA Affiliate listed in the white pages of your telephone book, the resources listed below may offer important additional services and/or information.

For the visually challenged:

American Council of the Blind
1155 15th Street, NW
Suite 720
Washington, DC 20005
(202) 467-5081
(800) 424-8666
National information clearinghouse and legislative advocate that publishes a bimonthly newsletter in Braille, large print, and cassette versions.

American Foundation for the Blind
15 West 16th Street
New York, NY 10011
(212) 620-2000
(800) 232-5463
Works to establish, develop, and provide services and programs that assist visually challenged people in achieving independence.

American Printing House for the Blind
1839 Frankfort Avenue
PO Box 6085
Louisville, KY 40206
(502) 895-2405
Concerned with the publication of literature in all media (Braille, large type, recorded) and manufacture of educational aids. Newsletter provides information on new products.

Division for the Blind and Visually Impaired
Rehabilitation Service Administration
U.S. Department of Education
Room 3229
Mary Switzer Building
330 C Street, SW
Washington, DC 20202
(202) 205-9309

Provides rehabilitation services, through agencies in each state, to those who have become visually impaired who wish to maintain their employment or train for new employment.

National Association for Visually Handicapped
(NAVH)
22 West 21st Street
New York, NY 10010
(212) 889-3141
or
NAVH San Francisco regional office (for states west of the Mississippi)
3201 Balboa Street
San Francisco, CA 94121
(415) 221-3201
List of low-vision facilities available by state. Visual aid counseling and visual aids, peer support groups, and more intensive counseling offered at two offices. Some counseling done by mail or phone.

National Federation of the Blind
1800 Johnson Street
Baltimore, MD 21230
(410) 659-9314 (for general information)
(800) 638-7518 (toll-free number only for job opportunities for the blind)
Membership organization providing information, networking and resources through 52 affiliates in all states, D.C. and Puerto Rico. Some aids and appliances available through national headquarters. The Diabetics Division publishes a free quarterly newsletter, Voice of the Diabetic, in print or on cassette.

National Library Service (NLS) for the Physically Handicapped
Library of Congress
1291 Taylor Street, NW
Washington, DC 20542

(202) 707-5100
(800) 424-8567 (to speak with a reference person)
(800) 424-9100 (to leave a message)
Encore, a monthly magazine on flexible disc (record), includes articles from *Diabetes Forecast*. It is available on request through the NLS program to individuals registered with talking book program.

Recordings for the Blind (RFB)
20 Roszel Road
Princeton, NJ 08540
(609) 452-0606 (voice)
(609) 987-8116 (fax)
(800) 221-4792 (weekdays 9-9 EST)
Audiotape library for the print-handicapped registered with RFB. Free loan of cassettes for up to a year. 80,000 titles on cassette.

Seeing Eye Guide Dogs
PO Box 375
Morristown, NJ 07963-0375
(201) 539-4425 (voice)
(201) 539-0922 (fax)
Guide dog training and instruction on working with a guide dog.

For amputees:

American Amputee Foundation
PO Box 250218
Little Rock, AR 72225
(501) 666-2523
Assists in removing workplace barriers for amputees. Peer counseling to new amputees and their families. Information and referral. Has local chapters.

National Amputation Foundation
73 Church Street
Malverne, NY 11565

(516) 887-3600 (voice)
(516) 887-3667 (fax)
Sponsor of Amp-to-Amp program in which new amputee is visited by amputee who has resumed normal life. List of support groups throughout the country available.

For those needing long-term or home care:

National Association for Home Care (NHAC)
519 C Street, NE
Washington, DC 20002-5809
(202) 547-7424
Free information for consumers about how to choose a home care agency. Send self-addressed stamped envelope.

Nursing Home Information Service
c/o National Council of Senior Citizens
1331 F Street, NW
Washington, DC 20004
(202) 347-8800
Information on selecting and paying for a nursing home.

Sources for finding quality health care:

American Medical Association
515 North State Street
Chicago, IL 60610
(312) 464-4818
Will tell you how to contact your county or state medical society, which will provide you with a referral to a local physician.

American Board of Medical Specialties
1 Rotary Center, Suite 805
Evanston, IL 60201
(708) 491-9091

(800) 776-2378
Record of physicians certified by 24 medical specialty
boards. Certification status of physician available to
callers. Directories of certified physicians organized
by city of medical practice and alphabetically by
physician names available in many libraries.

American Association for Marriage and Family
Therapy
1100 17th Street, NW, 10th Floor
Washington, DC 20036
(202) 452-0109
(800) 374-2638
Referral to local professional marriage and family
therapist.

National Association of Social Workers
750 First Street, NE
Suite 700
Washington, DC 20002
(202) 408-8600
(800) 638-8799
Referral to local professional social worker.

American Association of Diabetes Educators
444 North Michigan Avenue, Suite 1240
Chicago, IL 60611
(312) 644-2233
(800) 338-3633
Referral to local professional diabetes educator.

The American Dietetic Association
216 West Jackson Boulevard, Suite 800
Chicago, IL 60606
(312) 899-0040
(800) 366-1655
Information, guidance, and referral to local professional dietitian plus Consumer Nutrition Hotline.

American Optometric Association
243 N. Lindbergh Boulevard
St. Louis, MO 63141
(314) 991-4100
Referral to state optometric association for local referral to professional optometrists.

American Board of Podiatric Surgery
1601 Dolores Street
San Francisco, CA 94110
(415) 826-3200
Referral to board-certified local podiatrist.

For miscellaneous health information:

American Academy of Ophthalmology
Customer Service Department
PO Box 7424
San Francisco, CA 94120-7424
(415) 561-8500
For brochures on eye care and eye diseases, send a self-addressed, stamped envelope.

American Heart Association
(800) 242-8721
For referral to local affiliate's Heartline, which provides information on cardiovascular health and disease prevention.

Avenues Unlimited Inc.
1199-K Avenida Acaso
Camarillo, CA 93012
(800) 848-2837 or from Canada call collect to (805) 484-8138
For a catalog of clothing designed for people in wheelchairs or with limited mobility.

Impotence Institute of America
(800) 669-1603
For information, guidance, and physician referral in
each state on impotence.

Medic Alert Foundation
PO Box 1009
Turlock, CA 95381-1009
(800) 432-5378
To order a medical ID bracelet.

National Kidney Foundation
30 E. 33rd Street
New York, NY 10016
(800) 622-9010
For donor cards and information about transplants.

National AIDS Hotline
(800) 342-2437 (24-hour)
(800) 344-7432 (Spanish)
(800) 243-7889 (TDD)
Information, counseling and referral on issues of HIV
and AIDS.

National Chronic Pain Outreach Association
7979 Old Georgetown Road, Suite 100
Bethesda, MD 20814
(301) 652-4948 (phone)
(301) 907-0745 (fax)
To learn more about chronic pain and how to deal
with it.

Prescription Footwear Association
9861 Broken Land Parkway, Suite 255
Columbia, MD 21046-1151
(800) 673-8447
Provides referrals to local certified pedorthists (people trained in fitting prescription footwear).

For travelers:

To order *Health Information for International Travelers*:
Centers for Disease Control, U.S. Government
Printing Office, stock no. 017-023-00192-2
Superindtendent of Documents
P.O. Box 371954
Pittsburgh PA 15250-7954
(202) 783-3238
Order by credit card by phone or send check or
money order for $6.50. 1993 edition available.

For a list of doctors in foreign countries who speak
English and who received postgraduate training in
North America or Great Britain:
International Association for Medical Assistance to
Travelers
417 Center Street
Lewiston, NY 14092
(716) 754-4883

For a list of International Diabetes Federation groups
that can offer assistance when you're traveling:
International Diabetes Federation
40 Washington Street
B-1050 Brussels, Belgium

For exercisers:

International Diabetic Athletes Association
6829 North 12th Street, Suite 205
Phoenix, AZ 85014
(602) 230-8155
For people with diabetes interested in sports at all levels, as well as health-care professionals. Newsletter.

President's Council on Physical Fitness
(202) 272-3430
For a free copy of *One Step at a Time*, a information

guide on running.

American College of Sports Medicine
P.O. Box 1440
Indianapolis, IN 46206-1440
(317) 637-9200

For people over 50:

American Association for Retired Persons (AARP)
601 E Street, NW
Washington, DC 20049
(202) 434-2277
Pharmacy (800) 456-2277
Prescriptions mailed to your door. Prices the same for members and nonmembers. $1 postage and shipping per order. Possible savings over drugstore prices on generic drugs, but no prices are guaranteed.

National Council on the Aging
409 3rd Street, 2nd Floor
Washington, DC 20024
(202) 479-1200
(800) 424-9047
Advocacy group concerned with developing and implementing high standards of care for the elderly. Referral to local agencies concerned with the elderly.

For equal employment information:

Equal Employment Opportunity Commission
For technical assistance and filing a charge:
(800) 669-4000
For publications on the Americans with Disabilities Act:
(800) 669-3362
(800) 800-3302 (TDD)

American Bar Association
Commission on Mental and Physical Disability Law
1800 M Street, NW
Washington, DC 20036
(2020) 331-2240
Provides information and technical assistance on all aspects of disability law.

Disability Rights Education and Defense Fund, Inc.
2212 6th Street
Berkeley, CA 94710
(510) 644-2555 (Voice/TDD)
Provides technical assistance and information to employers and individuals with disabilities on disability rights legislation and policies. Assists with legal representation.

National Information Center for Children and Youth with Disabilities
P.O. Box 1492
Washington, DC 20013
(703) 893-6061 (Voice)
(703) 893-8614 (TDD)
(800) 999-5599 (Voice)
Maintains database containing up-to-date information on disability topics.

Health insurance information:

Social Security Administration
(800) 772-1213

Medicare Hotline
(800) 638-6833

National Insurance Consumer Organization
P.O. Box 15492
Alexandria, VA 22309
(703) 549-8050

National Insurance Consumer Helpline
(800) 942-4242

The Medicare Handbook is available from:
Medicare Publications
Health Care Financing Administration
6325 Security Boulevard
Baltimore, MD 21207

Free Medicare/Medicaid counseling referral services
from the AARP:
(202) 434-2241

Health insurance through the AARP:
(800) 523-5800
The AARP administers 10 health insurance plans. For some plans, individuals with diabetes or other chronic illnesses are eligible within six months after enrolling in Medicare Part B. For other plans, a 3-month waiting period is required for those with conditions preexistent in the 6 months preceding the effective date of the insurance.

State Insurance Departments
   You may need to contact your state's insurance department if you have questions about insurance policy options within your state.   If you want to report a complaint because your insurer has denied a claim, you should also contact the insurance department.
   Some states have formed insurance risk pools to make it possible for individuals to obtain health insurance regardless of their state of health. In the list below, states are divided according to whether they do or do not have risk-pooled insurance. Some of the states with risk pools may have stopped accepting new members temporarily or permanently.   Check with the insurance department. If your state is not

listed as having risk-pooled insurance, check with your state's insurance department as well. Some states may have adopted such an insurance program since March 31, 1994.

Calls to an 800 number listed below are free when made within the state.

States with insurance risk pools as of March 31, 1994:

Alaska
Division of Insurance
800 E. Dimond, Suite 560
Anchorage, AK 99515
(907) 349-1230

California
Insurance Department
Consumer Services Division
300 S. Spring Street
Los Angeles, CA 90013
(213) 346-6500
(800) 927-4357

Colorado
Insurance Division
1560 Broadway
Suite 850
Denver, CO 80202
(303) 894-7499, ext. 356

Connecticut
Insurance Department
PO Box 816
Hartford, CT 06142-0816
(203) 297-3800
(800) 842-0004

Florida
Department of Insurance
200 East Gaines Street
Tallahassee, FL 32399-0322
(904) 922-3100
(800) 342-2762

Georgia
7th Floor, West Tower
2 Martin Luther King, Jr., Drive
716 West Tower
Atlanta, GA 30334
(404) 656-2056

Illinois
Insurance Department
320 West Washington Street
Springfield, IL 62767
(217) 782-4515

Indiana
Insurance Department
311 West Washington, Suite 300
Indianapolis, IN 46204-2787
(317) 232-2385
(800) 622-4461

Iowa
Insurance Division
Lucas State Office Building
E. 12th & Grand Sts.
6th Floor
Des Moines, IA 50319
(515) 281-5705
(800) 877-5156

Louisiana
Insurance Department
PO Box 94214

Baton Rouge, LA 70804
(504) 342-5900

Maine
Bureau of Insurance
Consumer Division
State House, Station 34
Augusta, ME 04333
(207) 582-8707

Minnesota
Insurance Department
Department of Commerce
133 E. 7th Street
St. Paul, MN 55101-2362
(612) 296-2788

Mississippi
Insurance Department
Consumer Assistance Division
PO Box 79
Jackson, MS 39205
(601) 359-3569

Missouri
Department of Insurance
Consumer Services Section
PO Box 690
Jefferson City, MO 65102-0690
(314) 751-2640
(800) 726-7390

Montana
Department of Insurance
Mitchell Building, PO Box 4009
Helena, MT 59604-4009
(406) 444-2040

Nebraska
Insurance Department
Terminal Building
941 "O" Street, Suite 400
Lincoln, NE 68508
(402) 471-2201

New Mexico
Department of Insurance
PO Drawer 1269
Sante Fe, NM 87504-1269
(505) 827-4500

North Dakota
600 East Boulevard
Bismarck, ND 58505-0158
(701) 224-2440
(800) 247-0560

Oregon
Department of Insurance
21 Labor & Industries
Building
Salem, OR 97310
(503) 378-4271

Rhode Island
Insurance Division
233 Richmond Street, Suite
233
Providence, RI 02903-4233
(401) 277-2223

South Carolina
Department of Insurance
Consumer Services Section
PO Box 100105
Columbia, SC 29202-3105
(803) 737-6180
(800) 768-3467

South Dakota
Insurance Department
500 E. Capitol Avenue
Pierre, SD 57501-5070
(605) 773-3563

Tennessee
Department of Commerce and
Insurance
Insurance Assistance Office
4th Floor
500 James Robertson Parkway
Nashville, TN 37243
(615) 741-4955
(800) 525-2816

Texas
Department of Insurance
Consumer Protection (111-1A)
P.O. Box 149091
Austin, TX 78714-9091
(512) 463-6515
(800) 252-3439

Utah
Insurance Department
Consumer Services
3110 State Office Building
Salt Lake City, UT 84114-
1201
(801) 538-3800
(800) 439-3805

Washington
Insurance Department
Insurance Building
P.O. Box 40255
Olympia, WA 98504-0255
(206) 753-7300
(800) 562-6900

Wisconsin
Insurance Department
Complaints Department
PO Box 7873
Madison, WI 53707-7873
(608) 266-3585
(800) 236-8517

Wyoming
Insurance Department
Herschler Building
122 West 25th Street
Cheyenne, WY 82002-0440
(307) 777-7401
(800) 438-5768

States without insurance risk pools as of August 1, 1991:

Alabama
Insurance Department
Consumer Services Division
135 South Union Street
Montgomery, AL 36130-3351
(205) 269-3550

Arizona
Insurance Department
Consumer Affairs Division
2910 N. 44th Street
Phoenix, AZ 85018
(602) 912-8440

Arkansas
Insurance Department
1123 S. University Ave.
400 University Tower Building
Little Rock, AR 72204

(501) 686-2900
(800) 852-5494

Delaware
Insurance Department
Rodney Building
841 Silver Lake Boulevard
Dover, DE 19901
(302) 736-4251
(800) 282-8611

District of Columbia
Insurance Department
613 G Street, NW
Room 638
Washington, DC 20001
(202) 727-8009

Hawaii
Dpartment of Commerce &
    Consumer Affairs
Insurance Division
PO Box 3614
Honolulu, HI 96811
(808) 586-2790

Idaho
Insurance Department
Public Service Department
700 West State Street
Boise, ID 83720
(208) 334-4320

Kansas
Insurance Department
420 S.W. 9th Street
Topeka, KS 66612
(913) 296-3071
(800) 432-2484

Kentucky
Insurance Department
229 West Main Street
Frankfort, KY 40602
(502) 564-3630

Maryland
Insurance Administration
Complaints and
Investigation Unit-
  Life and Health
501 St. Paul Place
Baltimore, MD 21202-2272
(301) 333-2793

Massachusetts
Insurance Division
Consumer Services Section
470 Atlantic Ave.
Boston, MA 02210-2223
(617) 521-7777

Michigan
Insurance Bureau
P.O. Box 30220
Ottawa Building North, 2nd
Floor
Lansing, MI 48909
(517) 373-0240

Nevada
Department of Business and
Industry
Division of Insurance
1665 Hot Springs Road, Ste.
152
Carson City, NV 89710
(702) 486-4009
(800) 992-0900

New Hampshire
Insurance Department
Life and Health Division
GAA Plaza, 169 Manchester
Street
Concord, NH 03301
(603) 271-2261
(800) 852-3416

New Jersey
Insurance Department
20 West State Street
Roebling Building
CN-325
Trenton, NJ 08625-0325
(609) 292-5363

New York
Insurance Department
Consumer Affairs
160 West Broadway
New York, NY 10013
(212) 602-0203
(800) 342-3736

North Carolina
Insurance Department
PO Box 26387
Raleigh, NC 27611
(919) 733-7343
(800) 662-7777

Ohio
Insurance Department
Consumer Services Division
2100 Stella Court
Columbus, OH 43266-0566
(614) 644-2673
(800) 686-1526

Oklahoma
Insurance Department
PO Box 53408
Oklahoma City, OK 73152-3408
(405) 521-6628

Pennsylvania
Insurance Department
Consumer Services Bureau
1321 Strawberry Square
Harrisburg, PA 17120
(717) 787-2317

Puerto Rico
Office of the Commissioner of
Insurance
P.O. Box 8330
San Juan, PR 00910-8330
(809) 722-8686

Vermont
Department of Banking,
Insurance and Securities
Consumer Complaints Division
89 Main Street, Drawer 20
Montpelier, VT 05620-3101
(802) 828-3301

Virginia
Bureau of Insurance
Consumer Services Division
1300 East Main Street
P.O. Box 1157
Richmond, VA 23209
(804) 371-9741
(800) 552-7945

West Virginia
Insurance Department
Consumer Services Division
2019 Washington Street East
Charleston, WV 25305
(304) 348-3394
(800) 642-9004

To Order Books From ADA
Now that you're taking charge of your diabetes, take a look at our complete library of self-care and meal-planning books. Use the order form at the right, or give us a call.

Order Toll-Free!
1-800-232-3472
MasterCard, VISA,
American Express

___Yes! Please send me the books I've chosen, and include a free catalog.

Item #	Title	Qty	Unit Price	Total

Subtotal $_____
VA residents add 4.5% sales tax $_____
Shipping & Handling (see chart) $_____
GRAND TOTAL $_____

Name _____
Address _____
City/State/Zip _____
CH694T1
___ Payment enclosed (check or money order) OR
_____VISA _____MasterCard _____ American Express
Account Number:_____Expires _____
Signature: _____

Shipping & Handling
up to $30.......add $3.00
$30.01-$50.00...add $4.00
over $50.00.....add 8%

Allow 2–3 weeks for shipment. Add $3 to shipping & handling for each extra shipping address. Add $15 for each overseas shipment. Prices subject to change without notice. Foreign orders must be paid in U.S. funds, drawn on a U.S. bank.

Mail to: American Diabetes Association
              1970 Chain Bridge Road
              McLean, VA 22109-0592
or call   (800) 232-3472

Index